DEATH AND THE AFTERLIFE

The Bible Speaks

"Have the gates of death been opened unto thee?
or hast thou seen the doors of the shadow of death?"
Job 38:17

Leroy Freeman

DEATH AND THE AFTERLIFE
The Bible Speaks

All Scripture quotations are taken from the **King James Version** of the Holy Bible, except where otherwise noted.

For information, write: **Permissions**
Rejoice Printing
P.O. Box 221076
West Palm Beach, FL 33422

ISBN 978-0-9822739-3-7

Published by: Rejoice Printing - a publishing ministry of
Leroy Freeman Evangelistic Association
dba/More Than Conquerors

Cover design by Leroy Freeman

P.O. Box 221076 ~ West Palm Beach, FL 33422 USA

Printed in the United States of America

Dedication

This book is dedicated to my three beautiful children and their families, LeRoy Freeman, Jr. ~ Angel Freeman Wilson ~ and Gabriel Freeman.

Grace, mercy, and peace be with you always as you continue to strive to walk in God's ways and fulfill His calling upon your lives.

God bless you!

Acknowledgements

Many thanks to the love of my life, my beautiful, precious wife, Patricia A. Meadows Freeman for her much needed assistance in the writing of this book.

I am very grateful for her late nights of untiring dedication and expertise in proofreading and critiquing the book. Also, I appreciate her probing questions and many suggestions in helping to make this book as easy to read and as simple as possible for the reader.

Trish (Cuppie), may God continue to richly bless and use you for His glory. Love ya

Also, I would like to thank Angel Freeman Wilson and Christine March for helping to proofread this book.

Contents

Foreword

Evangelist Leroy Freeman has written an excellent Bible review on the subject of Death and the Afterlife.

As a pastor, I can recommend this study for both individuals and groups. After reviewing Jewish teaching on death and the afterlife, Evangelist Leroy Freeman presents Jesus' teachings.

It is very clear that Jesus promises those who accept Him as Lord and Savior, a place in the Father's heavenly kingdom,

"In My Father's house there are many rooms,
and I go to prepare a place for you."

"This day you shall be with Me in Paradise."

These are but two of the verses where Jesus promises His disciples a place with the Father. Evangelist Freeman discusses all the places where Jesus refers to death and our place in Paradise. His analysis and insights are very helpful to even the professional reader.

This is an exhaustive study of the subject based on what the Scriptures say. Reading this book will truly help one prepare to present what the Scriptures say about death and the afterlife.

Dr. Albert W. Bush, Jr.
Founding Pastor
Gardens Presbyterian Church
Palm Beach Gardens, FL

Introduction

Death is one of the things in life that remains certain. Since the dawn of history, the subject of death and the afterlife has been the great mystery of human existence. This is a subject of universal interest that everyone wonders about.

Death cares not whether we are rich, poor, male, or female. Death does not care about what race we are or if we have been good or bad. Death can come through old age, illness, accident, violence, or any number of ways. One way or another, we all die. Death is the only event which we can predict with absolute certainty. According to the latest figures, apart from Enoch and Elijah, the death rate is still 100%.

At different times, we each think about death. At other times we seek to avoid it by preoccupation or pursuit of other things. Even if we would rather avoid the topic, death will not avoid us. We (all) must pass through the doorway of death at some point in time, when we leave this earth.

Inquiries about dying, death, and the afterlife continue to be one of the most popular searches on the Internet. Many hate to think about death and the afterlife because the prospect of what they may face after death can be quite horrifying.

Death marks a point of transition, whereby we let go of everything and everyone that we love on this side. We *then* pass from one well known stage or realm of life into another veiled mysterious one. At the point of death (without faith) this can be an extremely difficult time of loneliness, sadness, curiosity, and fear.

There is great confusion concerning death and the afterlife. There are many sources that speak on the subject; some are trustworthy and some are not. Scientists, philosophers, religions, and even within the Christian faith, there is much confusion and disagreement regarding what happens at death and what happens in the afterlife.

All kinds of books, television shows, and groups are fostering unbiblical views of life after death. Many use works of fiction - Mythology, Christian novels, Comic books, etc.- to rely on for their theology. In some of these resources, you see red devils and demons ruling in Hell with pitchforks sticking people. You also see some who are expected to be reincarnated, coming back to the earth as another person or as an animal.

There are many other popular myths about death that are also generated. Time and time again, out comes *new light* about death and the afterlife which lasts for a while and fades; then, out comes other theories of *new light*. This happens when opinions, ideas, and guesstimates are offered apart from what has been revealed in the Scriptures.

God alone knows the answers to the mysteries of life and death. Only God can supply the answers we so desperately need and He reveals them to us in His Word, the Holy Bible.

In Scripture, everything is not easy to understand and interpret. We (only) know what Christ and the Holy Spirit have revealed to us. What divides us is what has not been said. When we attempt to fill in the gaps and attempt to clarify or clear up those things which the Lord leaves unclear, this is when we separate.

If there are gaps about death and the afterlife that have not been filled in by the Lord – let's leave it that way. It was God's will to do it that way, so we would walk by faith and trust Him in matters that are difficult to understand.

The Good News is that death doesn't have to be a mystery nor be entirely devastating. God has not left us without hope. He has given us more than enough in His Word to comfort us concerning death and the afterlife.

I pray this book ~ Death and The Afterlife (The Bible Speaks) ~ helps in untwisting some of the twisted teachings concerning life's greatest mystery.

Evangelist Leroy Freeman

∽ 1 ∾

Questions Concerning Death and The Afterlife

Concerning death and the afterlife, there are many questions that people of distant times have been concerned with. Four thousand years ago, in the midst of tragic suffering and death, Job asked a couple of questions about death by saying,

"But man dieth, and wasteth away:
yea, man giveth up the ghost, and where is he?
If a man die, shall he live again?"
Job 14:10,14

The Psalmist also had questions:

"Wilt thou show wonders to the dead?
Shall the dead arise and praise thee? Selah.
Shall thy lovingkindness be declared in the grave?
Or thy faithfulness in destruction?"
Psalm 88:10,11

For the many complicated questions about death and the afterlife – apart from the Bible, there are no real answers. God's Word is the only source that makes the teaching clear. It is the Handbook we need that lets us know what is beyond death's door, and also helps us prepare for the ages of ages to come. Through the Word of God, we can learn much about both death, and the afterlife.

These are just a few of the questions surrounding death which people have asked and pondered since the beginning of earthly time.

- Do we have an appointed time of death?
- How exactly is death defined in Scripture?
- What lies behind the veil of death?
- Where do we go when we die?
- Do we have immortal souls?
- Are we conscious after we die?
- What is the afterlife like?
- In what state will believers exist?
- What will our physical bodies look like?
- Do we lose all sense of personal identity and recognition?
- Will we remember our earthly lives in Heaven?
- Will we know loved ones who have passed on before?
- What will we do in eternity?
- What does the Bible say about Purgatory?
- Is there a place called Hell?
- Are there different levels of punishment in Hell?
- How can I not go to Hell?
- Will we experience some form of reward?
- What are the Heavenly Crowns?
- Do we immediately go to Heaven, Hell, or somewhere in-between?

These are serious questions, but if one studies and believes what the Bible says, many of these questions can be answered without confusion or contradiction. There are also many other questions about death and the afterlife that are not easy to interpret and are incapable of being answered by us in this life, even with a thorough knowledge of the Hebrew (Old Testament) and Greek (New Testament) languages which were used for the translation of the King James Version of the Holy Bible. Some things we will not know, until we reach the other side. The Scripture says,

"The secret things belong unto the Lord our God:
but those things which are revealed belong
unto us and to our children for ever ... ."
Deuteronomy 29:29

Apostle Paul said,

"For now we see through a glass, darkly; but then face to face:
now I know in part; but then shall I know even as also I am known."
I Corinthians 13:12

As we examine many of these topics – we have already been warned by the Word of God not to add or take anything away from His Word.

"... If any man shall add unto these things,
God shall add unto him the plagues that are written in this Book:
And if any man shall take away from the words of the Book of this Prophecy,
God shall take away his part out of the Book of Life, and out of the Holy City,
and from the things which are written in this Book."
Revelation 22:18,19

We know (only) what Christ and the saints have revealed to us by the Holy Spirit.

There are many who have had Near Death Experiences and have testified to have died and come back to life. Concerning these great stories which are told (as we listen to these death and near death experiences), we must weigh everything that's said by the Word of God. Every experience must fit within the boundaries of Scripture.

Some people seem to have all the answers and appear to be able to fill in all the gaps. However, since God said in Deuteronomy 29:29 - "the secret things belong unto the Lord our God." Concerning some things, we will never have total clarity. For this reason, we must stay with God's Word and say (only) what it says and what God has chosen to reveal in Scripture concerning death and the afterlife.

New age teachings and all sorts of interpretations come and go with the winds of time, but truth remains steadfast and eternal. This is why our omniscient God instructs us in Scripture to,

"Prove all things... ."
I Thessalonians 5:21

There's no better way to prove the things that I say and believe, other than by the Word of God. Let's get the truth - not theories, not opinions, not personal beliefs, but TRUTH.

As Jesus stood before the Governor,

"Pilate saith unto Him, What is truth? .... "
John 18:38

Jesus responded,

"... Thy [God's] Word is truth."
John 17:17

Let's look into God's holy, inspired Word, and see what our Creator says about death and the afterlife.

Knowing the answers to many of the questions that are asked about death and the afterlife gives us hope and will help determine the way we live and interact with life. It will also help us find peace and joy and will actively influence the way we approach the dying process.

Test Your Knowledge

*** All answers to the following questions can be found within the pages of this chapter or the Answer Key (at the back of the book).

CHALLENGE YOURSELF: Test your knowledge without referring to the Answer Key

Chapter 1 – Questions Concerning Death and the Afterlife

1. Deuteronomy 29:29 tells us that "the ____________ things belong unto the Lord our God: but those things which are ____________ belong unto us and to our children forever."

2. Who asked the question, "If a man die, shall he live again?"
   a. David
   b. Job
   c. Paul
   d. Peter

3. What chapter and verse applies to question #2?
   a. Psalm 88:10
   b. Job 14:10
   c. Job 14:14
   d. Peter 1:3

4. _____________ remains steadfast and eternal.

5. New age teachings and all sorts of interpretations come and go with the winds of time. We are told in Scripture to, "__________ _______ things." I Thess. 5:_____

6. As Jesus stood before the Governor, who said to Him ..."What is truth?"

   a. Caesar

   b. Caiaphas

   c. Pilate

   d. A Pharisee

7. According to Jesus in John 17:____, what did He say was "Truth"?

8. The King James Version's translation of the Bible's (Old Testament and New Testament) was translated using how many languages?

   a. 3

   b. 1

   c. 4

   d. 2

9. The King James Version of the Bible's Old Testament was translated from which language(s)?

   a. Greek

   b. Latin

   c. Hebrew

   d. English

   e. Two of the above

10. The King James Version of the Bible's New Testament was translated from the Greek language?

    a. True

    b. False

HOW WELL DID YOU DO?

GRADE SCALE

Missed 0 = Excellent
Missed 1 = Very Good
Missed 2 = Good
Missed 3 = Average
Mised 4 or more = Need to Re-read Chapter

☐ Excellent
☐ Very Good
☐ Good
☐ Average
☐ Need to Re-read Chapter

2

Where Did Death Come From?

For the answer to this question, we must go back to the beginning to the Biblical account of the first human being and follow the steps of how death came on the scene of human existence.

"And God said, Let us make man in our image,
after our likeness: and let them have dominion over the fish of the sea,
and over the fowl of the air, and over the cattle, and over all the earth,
and over every creeping thing that creepeth upon the earth."
Genesis 1:26

"And the Lord God formed man of the dust of the ground,
and breathed into his nostrils the breath of life;
and man became a living soul."
Genesis 2:7

"And the Lord God planted a garden eastward in Eden;
and there He put the man whom He had formed.
And out of the ground made the Lord God to grow every tree
that is pleasant to the sight, and good for food;
the Tree of Life also in the midst of the garden,
and the Tree of Knowledge of Good and Evil."
Genesis 2:8,9

After they were made, Adam and Eve were placed in a beautiful garden that God planted.

"And the Lord God took the man, and put him into the Garden of Eden to dress it and to keep it."
Genesis 2:15

The Creator made Himself responsible for meeting bountifully every need of His creatures.

First Mention of Death

In the beginning, it was God who first mentioned death.

"And the Lord God commanded the man, saying, Of every tree of the garden thou mayest freely eat: But of the Tree of the Knowledge of Good and Evil, thou shalt not eat of it: for in the day that thou eatest thereof thou shalt surely die."
Genesis 2:16,17

God personally instructed them not to eat of the Tree of the Knowledge of Good and Evil or they would surely die.

Adam and Eve had all they needed in the garden. They had fellowship with God. Righteousness ruled, therefore, peace resulted. There was nothing to hinder perfect obedience to the will of God.

Would Adam and Eve accept this limitation and be content to stay wholly within the circle of God's will, or would they exercise their will in a choice contrary to the will of God? There would be only one way to know, and that would be through the way of a test. God gave the command. Adam and Eve were to make the choice - to obey or disobey.

Satan, who was also in the Garden of Eden, appeared to Eve through a serpent and asked if she was permitted to take of the fruit of the Tree of the Knowledge of Good and Evil. Her reply was,

"And the woman said unto the serpent, We may eat of the fruit of the trees of the garden: But of the fruit of the tree which is in the midst of the garden, God hath said, Ye shall not eat of it, neither shall ye touch it, lest ye die."
Genesis 3:2,3

"And the serpent said unto the woman, Ye shall not surely die:
For God doth know that in the day ye eat thereof, then your eyes
shall be opened, and ye shall be as gods, knowing good and evil."
Genesis 3:4,5

Satan contradicted God by saying to Eve, "ye shall not surely die" and caused her to doubt God's Word. Satan also caused her to think that God was keeping something desirable from them by saying, *"God doth know that ye shall be as gods."*

Eve fell for Satan's trick and believed the serpent's lie. She ate of the forbidden fruit and also persuaded Adam to disobey God. The moment they ate of that fruit, they felt different about themselves and about God. Their inner eyes were opened, they were ashamed of their nakedness, and wanted to hide from God.

"And the eyes of them both were opened,
and they knew that they were naked ... and
Adam and his wife hid themselves from the presence
of the Lord God amongst the trees of the garden."
Genesis 3:7,8

The very moment Adam and Eve ate of the forbidden fruit, they had knowledge of good and evil, but it was not what they expected. The innocent, trusting relationship they had with God was destroyed. Just as God had said, the death sentence came upon them.

Since Adam's physical life did not end on the first day he sinned, we know that God's definition of death transcends ours.

Scripture clearly shows that there are three deaths:

- Physical
- Spiritual
- Eternal (Second).

1. **Spiritual Death** - The moment Adam sinned by eating of the forbidden fruit, he died spiritually. Paul describes our spiritual state as being,

"... dead in trespasses and sin."
Ephesians 2:1

2. Physical Death - the same day that Adam sinned his body began to age, even though he did not die physically until many years later.

"And all the days that Adam lived
were nine hundred and thirty years: and he died."
Genesis 5:5

As stated earlier, due to the death sentence that was activated by Adam and Eve's disobedience to God, we age and eventually we die. Then, our bodies return to dust. God said,

"... for dust thou art, and unto dust shalt thou return."
Genesis 3:19

Solomon said,

"... there is ... a time to be born and a time to die."
Ecclesiastes 3:1,2

The patriarch Job said concerning our time on earth,

"Seeing his days are determined, the number of his months are
with Thee, thou hast appointed his bounds that he cannot pass."
Job 14:5

3. Eternal (Second) Death – is being separated from the love and presence of God for all eternity.

"But the fearful, and unbelieving, and the abominable,
and murderers, and whoremongers, and sorcerers,
and idolaters, and all liars, shall have their part
in the lake which burneth with fire and brimstone:
which is the Second Death."
Revelation 21:8

Death is a separation. It was sin that caused death and separated man from God. Paul said,

"For the wages of sin is death .... "
Romans 6:23

Separation from God (Who is Life) is death, the result of Adam and Eve eating from the forbidden tree. This set in motion a world subject to the bondage of corruption; the physical process that ultimately leads to death for all living beings. The Scripture declares,

"For as in Adam all die .... "
I Corinthians 15:22

Because of the sin of disobedience, Adam and Eve caused innocent animals to die to provide them with coats of skin to cover their nakedness.

"Unto Adam also and to his wife did the Lord God
make coats of skins, and clothed them."
Genesis 3:21

Adam and Eve were then ejected from the Garden and forced to earn a living from a world cursed with thorns and thistles. The bondage of corruption had begun; even now, the whole creation continues to groan and travail in pain (crying out to be released from sin and suffering). The Apostle Paul said,

"For we know that the whole creation groaneth
and travaileth in pain together until now."
Romans 8:22

The New Living Translations says,

"Against its will, all creation was subjected to God's curse.
But with eager hope, the creation looks forward to the day when
it will join God's children in glorious freedom from death and decay.

For we know that all creation has been groaning
as in the pains of childbirth right up to the present time."
Romans 8:20-22 (NLT)

Test Your Knowledge

*** All answers to the following questions can be found within the pages of <u>this</u> chapter or the Answer Key (at the back of the book).

CHALLENGE YOURSELF: Test your knowledge without referring to the Answer Key

Chapter 2 – Where Did Death Come From?

1. Adam's job in the Garden of Eden was to ________ it and ________ it.

2. Name the tree Adam and Eve ate from that caused sin in the world.

   ____

3. Which fruit tree did God mention was forbidden?

   a. Peach

   b. Apple

   c. Orange

   d. None of the above

4. List the three deaths that resulted when Adam sinned by eating the forbidden fruit.

   a. ________________________

   b. ________________________

   c. ________________________

5. Who first mentioned death?
   a. Satan
   b. Adam
   c. God
   d. Serpent

6. Adam and Eve knew they were naked all the time.
   a. True
   b. False

7. What did "God" clothe Adam and Eve with?
   a. Fig leaves
   b. Apple leaves
   c. Coats of skins
   d. Palm Tree branches

8. Separation from God is death.
   a. True
   b. False

9. Since Adam's ____________ ____________ did not end on the first day he sinned, we know that God's definition of death transcends ours.

10. Satan contradicted God with Scripture.

   a. What did the serpent say unto the woman in Genesis 3 that contradicted what God said to Adam in Genesis 2?

   ____

   b. Which verse in Genesis 3 did the serpent use to contradict God?

   ______

HOW WELL DID YOU DO?

GRADE SCALE

Missed 0 = Excellent
Missed 1 = Very Good
Missed 2 = Good
Missed 3 = Average
Mised 4 or more = Need to Re-read Chapter

☐ Excellent
☐ Very Good
☐ Good
☐ Average
☐ Need to Re-read Chapter

3

Jesus' Victory Over Death

Adam's sin brought with it a heavy penalty. Since everybody is born into sin, everybody is subject to sin's penalty. The Apostle Paul says,

"For the wages of sin is death ... ."
Romans 6:23

It is the sinner who dies. Therefore, death has always been humanity's enemy. The Scripture points out mankind's inborn fear of death. The Hebrew writer tells us how Jesus came to,

"... deliver them who through fear of death were all their lifetime subject to bondage."
Hebrews 2:15

Death is not a pleasant subject. Growing up, I had a terrible fear of death and the afterlife. If you wanted me out of your presence, start talking about death and I would leave immediately. I knew on the inside that I was not ready to meet God and I didn't want to be faced with anything about my encounter with the Lord in the afterlife. Therefore, I buried my head in the sand about the subject of death, even though it was happening all around me.

It is crystal clear that God was not pleased with my attitude concerning death and the afterlife, because of what Jesus did in the above mentioned scripture in Hebrews chapter 2.

God is a Holy and loving God. He doesn't want us to be fearful concerning death, and He does not want anyone to perish. The Apostle Peter states,

"For the Lord is ... longsuffering to us-ward, not willing that any should perish, but that all should come to repentance."
2 Peter 3:9

A Holy God cannot change His attitude toward sin and His judgment upon it without denying His own nature. In order to provide a way of escape for the sinner, there must be an adequate substitute who would be able to meet the full penalty of the Law, voluntarily offer to take the sinner's place, and die the sinner's death.

There was only One who could meet those requirements. Because of God's love and mercy, He would give the best that He had for a bunch of sinners.

"For God so loved the world, that He gave His only begotten Son, that whosoever believeth in Him should not perish, but have everlasting life."
John 3:16

Two of the main purposes for the coming of Jesus Christ was to:

1. Destroy the works of the devil by conquering the power of death
2. Reconcile us back to God

The Scripture says,

"... For this purpose the Son of God was manifested, that He might destroy the works of the devil."
I John 3:8

"To wit, that God was in Christ, reconciling the world unto Himself ... ."
2 Corinthians 5:19

JESUS spoke often about death and dying. Christ's emphasis may have been on life, but a substantial portion of His messages dealt with death. His messages about death were not morbid or negative, but many of them were Gospel messages of good news about the triumphing of life over death. Jesus said of Himself,

"This is that bread which came down from heaven: not as your fathers did eat many, and are dead: he that eateth of this bread shall live for ever."
John 6:58

"Verily, verily, I say unto you, The hour is coming and now is when the dead shall hear the voice of the Son of God; and they that hear shall live."
John 5:25

Besides vigorously preaching this message, Jesus actually demonstrated in His earthly ministry what He will do in the future by calling the dead (bodies) back to life. Listed below are four examples reiterating this point.

1. Jesus added credibility (to the otherwise unbelievable) by raising up the twelve-year-old daughter of Jairus, who had just died.

"And He took the damsel by the hand, and said unto her, Talitha cumi; which is, being interpreted, Damsel, I say unto thee, arise. And straightway the damsel arose, and walked; for she was of the age of twelve years. And they were astonished with a great astonishment."
Mark 5:41,42

2. Jesus stopped the pallbearers at a young man's funeral and commanded the corpse to live again.

"And He came and touched the bier: and they that bare him stood still. And He said, Young man, I say unto thee, Arise. And he that was dead sat up, and began to speak. And He delivered him to his mother."
Luke 7:14,15

3. Jesus summoned Lazarus from the tomb after he had been dead and buried for four days.

"And when He thus had spoken, He cried with a loud voice, Lazarus, come forth. And he that was dead came forth, bound hand and foot with graveclothes: and his face was bound about with a napkin. Jesus saith unto them, Loose him, and let him go."
John 11:43,44

4. Jesus, who is the Resurrection and Life, allowed Himself to be publicly executed. Jesus said,

"Therefore doth My Father love Me, because I lay down My life, that I might take it again. No man taketh it from Me, but I lay it down of Myself. I have power to lay it down, and I have power to take it again."
John 10:17,18

After Jesus laid down His life, He was certified dead by Roman authorities, and buried in a sealed tomb guarded by soldiers.

"And Pilate marveled if He were already dead: and calling unto him the centurion, he asked him whether He had been any while dead. And when he knew it of the centurion, he gave the body to Joseph."
Mark 15:44,45

"So they went, and made the sepulchre sure, sealing the stone, and setting a watch."
Matthew 27:66

Even with the tomb closely guarded, three days later, Jesus arose from the dead. He returned after His victory over Death and Hell to state His case. Jesus said,

"I Am He that liveth, and was dead; behold, I am alive for evermore, Amen; and have the keys of Hell and of Death."
Revelation 1:18

Jesus showed Himself alive (in private and public appearances) to hundreds of people.

"Then saith He to Thomas, Reach hither thy finger, and behold My hands; and reach hither thy hand, and thrust it into My side: and be not faithless, but believing."
John 20:27

"Behold My hands and My feet, that it is I Myself: handle Me, and see; for a spirit hath not flesh and bones, as ye see Me have."
Luke 24:39

"... Christ died for our sins according to the Scriptures: And that He was seen of Cephas, then of the twelve: After that, He was seen of above five hundred brethren at once ... ."
I Corinthians 15:3-6

After being seen of them for 40 days after His resurrection, Jesus then ascended heavenward before the eyes of assembled witnesses. The Bible says,

"And when He had spoken these things, while they beheld, He was taken up; and a cloud received Him out of their sight.

And while they looked stedfastly toward Heaven as He went up, behold, two men stood by them in white apparel; Which also said, Ye men of Galilee, why stand ye gazing up into Heaven? This same Jesus, which is taken up from you into Heaven, shall so come in like manner as ye have seen Him go into Heaven."
Acts 1:9-11

The resurrection of Jesus Christ is one of the greatest miracles ever. Jesus died, was buried for three days, and then rose again. Jesus tells and shows us that there is life after death. The credibility of Jesus is sufficient.

As the disciples went forth into all the world, their main message was the Resurrection. This doctrine dominated all other doctrines of the afterlife.

"And with great power gave the apostles witness of the resurrection of the Lord Jesus: and great grace was upon them all."
Acts 4:33

After the disciples witnessed the resurrection of Jesus, they were no longer fearful and afraid. Because of Jesus, death had lost its sting and the threat of death had been swallowed up in victory.

The disciples, no longer ashamed of the message of victory over death, continued to speak boldly concerning the resurrection of the dead.

"And when they heard of the resurrection of the dead, some mocked: and others said, We will hear thee again of this matter."
Acts 17:32

As this scripture states, even though there were those who made fun of the message of the resurrection, many of them wanted to know more.

God does not want anyone to perish in Hell. He wants us all to spend eternity with Him. Christ's victory over death gave mankind the possibility that they too could conquer physical, spiritual, and eternal death, within their personal lives.

In order to do so, we simply need to receive God's free gift of forgiveness, by which we can be passed from death (eternal) unto life (eternal).

"Verily, verily, I say unto you, He that heareth My word, and believeth on Him that sent Me, hath everlasting life, and shall not come into condemnation; but is passed from death unto life."
John 5:24

To be passed from death to life, is a gift from God. We cannot earn it. There is no other way to get this Gift from God other than through Jesus Christ. Jesus said,

"I Am the Way, the Truth, and the Life
no man cometh unto the Father, but by Me."
John 14:6

Paul confirms the words of Jesus by saying,

"Neither is there salvation in any other, for there is none other name under Heaven given among men whereby we must be saved."
Acts 4:12

Even though life is temporary, death is not the end. God has not left us without hope. There is a greater purpose for living. Nothing compares to living for the Lord Jesus Christ.

"Thanks be unto God for His Unspeakable Gift."
2 Corinthians 9:15

Who would not want to embrace this wonderful hope? What a cause for rejoicing.

Test Your Knowledge

*** All answers to the following questions can be found within the pages of <u>this</u> chapter or the Answer Key (at the back of the book).

CHALLENGE YOURSELF: Test your knowledge without referring to the Answer Key

Chapter 3 – Jesus' Victory Over Death

1. What are the two main purposes for Jesus Christ coming into the world?

   a. ____

   b. ____

2. How old was Jairus' daughter that Jesus raised from the dead?

   a. 14

   b. 16

   c. 11

   d. 12

3. Jesus summoned Lazarus from the ________ after he had been ________ ________for ____ days.

4. "… He [Jesus] cried with a loud voice, Lazarus ________ ________. And he that was ________ ________ ____________, bound hand and foot with ____________________: and his face was bound about with a _________. Jesus saith unto them, ____________ ________, and let him go."

5. After Jesus arose, He was seen alive at one time by more than ________ brethren.

6. When Jesus arose, He had flesh and blood.

   a. True

   b. False

7. In reference to the Lord Jesus Christ, what kind of Gift did Paul thank God for?

   a. Precious

   b. Merciful

   c. Unspeakable

   d. Holy

8. Jesus was certified dead by ________________ authorities, and buried in a sealed tomb guarded by soldiers.

9. Even with the tomb closely guarded, three days later, Jesus arose from the dead, and showed Himself alive in ______________ to hundreds of people.

   a. Public and private places

   b. Ephesus

   c. Corinth

   d. Egypt

10. Jesus said, "I am He that liveth and was __________; behold I am __________ for evermore, Amen; and have the __________ of __________ and of __________."

11. What did Jesus say that we had to do to be "… passed from death unto life?"

    a. Hear the Word

    b. Be a good person

    c. Exude good karma

    d. Believe the Word

    e. a, d

    f. all of the above

12. In order to provide a way of escape for the sinner, list three things the Adequate Substitute had to do:

    a. ______________________________

    b. ______________________________

    c. ______________________________

GRADE SCALE

Missed 0 = Excellent
Missed 1 = Very Good
Missed 2 = Good
Missed 3 = Average
Mised 4 or more = Need to Re-read Chapter

HOW WELL DID YOU DO?

- ☐ Excellent
- ☐ Very Good
- ☐ Good
- ☐ Average
- ☐ Need to Re-read Chapter

4

Physical Death of The Body

According to Scripture, a human is a triune being, consisting of body, soul, and spirit. Paul said,

"... and I pray God your whole spirit and soul and body be preserved blameless unto the coming of our Lord Jesus Christ."
I Thessalonians 5:23

We are born corruptible and mortal. Our lives are physical. We live in a body, which in Scripture is called a tabernacle. One of the definitions of a tabernacle is a temporary dwelling place.

"For we know that if our earthly house of this tabernacle were dissolved, we have a building of God, an house not made with hands, eternal in the heavens."
2 Corinthians 5:1

Our physical body is a garment with which we are clothed for a while. It is full of limitations; oftentimes, it is a hindrance and a drag. This flesh is such a target for Satan and such an instrument of sin. It is the flesh that drags us down and brings us a thousand sorrows.

Unfortunately, for this poor old tabernacle, it constantly gets weak, tired, wounded, and damaged; liable at any moment to fall victim to sickness and disease. The older this tabernacle gets, the more it takes to keep it patched up and in a livable condition.

Therefore, Scripture portrays the body as groaning under its burden of weariness and weakness; crying out for the day of release.

"For we that are in this tabernacle do groan, being burdened:
not for that we would be unclothed, but clothed upon,
that mortality might be swallowed up of life."
2 Corinthians 5:4

The New Living Translation quotes this passage by saying,

"While we live in these earthly bodies, we groan and sigh,
but it's not that we want to die and get rid of these bodies
that clothe us. Rather, we want to put on our new bodies
so that these dying bodies will be swallowed up by life."
2 Corinthians 5:4 NLT

Through the salvation experience our souls are converted, but Christ has left our bodies (still to a large extent) in bondage; therefore, these bodies still have to suffer.

"And not only they, but ourselves also, which have the firstfruits
of the Spirit, even we ourselves groan within ourselves,
waiting for the adoption, to wit, the redemption of our body."
Romans 8:23

There comes a time for all of us to put off this mortal flesh, the process which is called death. Death terminates an individual's interaction with this physical dimension.

Science defines death as the stopping of the life function (i.e., all systems cease to operate—the heart stops circulating blood, the brain stops sending orders to the organs, all thought processes cease, the body becomes immobile, all regeneration processes stop, and the body starts to decay). At death when the cerebral functions cease; there is no more thought process, no reward, no memory, no knowledge, and no access to this world.

According to Scripture, there is no quarrel with the scientific definition here. The Bible defines physical death in the same way as science.

"Put not your trust in princes, nor in the son of man,
in whom there is no help. His breath goeth forth,
he returneth to his earth; in that very day his thoughts perish."
Psalm 146:3,4

"For the living know that they shall die: but the dead know not any thing, neither have they any more a reward; for the memory of them is forgotten. Whatsoever thy hand findeth to do, do it with thy might; for there is no work, nor device, nor knowledge, nor wisdom, in the grave, whither thou goest."
Ecclesiastes 9:5,10

Eventually, all living processes break down and cease.

"To every thing there is a season, and a time to every purpose under the heaven: A time to be born, and a time to die ... ."
Ecclesiastes 3:1,2

The Bible describes what happens at death to a human being's physical body, when we put off this mortal flesh. God says our bodies were made from the elements of the earth and they will return to these same elements after death. The Scripture says,

"In the sweat of thy face shalt thou eat bread, till thou return unto the ground; for out of it wast thou taken: for dust thou art, and unto dust shalt thou return."
Genesis 3:19

"All flesh shall perish together, and man shall turn again unto dust."
Job 34:15

What Is Death?

Death is a separation of the soul and spirit from the body.

"For as the body without the spirit is dead ... ."
James 2:26

In Scripture, the state of physical death is also called sleep.

"These things said He: and after that He saith unto them, Our friend Lazarus sleepeth; but I go, that I may awake him out of sleep. Then said His disciples, Lord, if he sleep, he shall do well.

Howbeit Jesus spake of his death; but they thought that He had spoken of taking of rest in sleep. Then said Jesus unto them plainly, Lazarus is dead."
John 11:11-14

The sleep of death is making reference (only) to the physical body. Just as normal sleep is temporary, so too is the death of the body. Even as sleep has its time of waking, death of the body will also have its time of awakening - which we call the resurrection.

"... but though the outward man would perish,
yet the inward man is renewed day by day."
2 Corinthians 4:16

Our bodies may be wasting away; however, there is more to the physical body than the visible elements from which it is made.

Test Your Knowledge

*** All answers to the following questions can be found within the pages of this chapter or the Answer Key (at the back of the book).

CHALLENGE YOURSELF: Test your knowledge without referring to the Answer Key

Chapter 4 – Physical Death of the Body

1. A human being has three parts: ___________, ___________, and ___________.

2. In Scripture, what is our physical body called?
   a. earthly house
   b. tabernacle
   c. outward man
   d. a , b, and c

3. In Scripture, the state of the physical body at death is called Sleep.
   a. True
   b. False

4. One of the definitions below does *NOT* refer to a tabernacle?
   a. Permanent dwelling place
   b. Building of God
   c. Temporary dwelling place
   d. Two of the above

5. What scripture refers to question #4? ____________________

6. Through the salvation experience our ______________ are converted, but Christ has left our ________________ in bondage.

7. Death _______________ an individual's interaction with this _______________dimension.

8. Even as sleep has its time of waking, death of the body will also have its time of awakening which we call the
   a. hibernation
   b. re-incarnation
   c. transmigration
   d. resurrection

9. Humans are born both incorruptible and mortal.
   a. True
   b. False

10. Mankind is not a triune being is a false statement because of verse ____ in 1 Thessalonians 5.

GRADE SCALE

Missed 0 = Excellent
Missed 1 = Very Good
Missed 2 = Good
Missed 3 = Average
Mised 4 or more = Need to Re-read Chapter

HOW WELL DID YOU DO?

☐ Excellent
☐ Very Good
☐ Good
☐ Average
☐ Need to Re-read Chapter

~ 5 ~

Soul ~ As Used In Scripture

God created a lifeless body in the form of man and gave it life by blowing air into its nostrils, making it a living soul. The Hebrew (Old Testament) word translated for *soul* in the following scriptures is *nephesh [neh'·fesh]*, and the Greek (New Testament) word is *psychē [psü-khā']* which means a breathing creature or animal. It also means the state of being alive.

"And the Lord God formed man of the dust of the ground, and breathed into his nostrils the breath of life; and man became a living soul."
Genesis 2:7

"The spirit of God has made me,
and the breath of the Almighty has given me life."
Job 33:4

According to Scripture, man is a triune being consisting of three parts.

"... and I pray God your whole spirit and soul and body be preserved blameless unto the coming of our Lord Jesus Christ."
I Thessalonians 5:23

There is a difference and a fine line between the soul and spirit. At times, it seems that Scripture interchanges the two. We often have problems when we try to distinguish the two. With our finite minds, making the division between the soul and the spirit often produces a challenge for us, especially when it comes to understanding death and the afterlife.

In contrast to our limited capabilities, the Word of God is able to separate or divide asunder the difference between the Soul and Spirit, as stated in the following Scripture.

"For the Word of God is quick, and powerful, and sharper than any twoedged sword, piercing even to the dividing asunder of soul and spirit ... ."
Hebrews 4:12

Soul in Scripture is used very often, but the word SOUL has many different meanings. In order to distinguish which definition is being referred to, we have to look at the context of Scripture in which it appears. Getting the wrong definition can lead to much confusion when it comes to an understanding of death and the afterlife.

Definitions Of "SOUL"

Here are a few instances of the word soul and the context in which it is used in Scripture.

I. Soul = Physical Life

"And it came to pass, as her soul was in departing, (for she died) that she called his name Benoni: but his father called him Benjamin."
Genesis 35:18

"... when thou shalt make His soul an offering for sin ... ."
Isaiah 53:10

"... He hath poured out His soul unto death ... ."
Isaiah 53:12

"Let him know, that he which converteth the sinner from the error of his way shall save a soul from death, and shall hide a multitude of sins."
James 5:20

II. Soul = People or Individuals

"Then they that gladly received His word were baptized: and the same day there were added unto them about three thousand souls."
Acts 2:41

"And we were all in the ship two hundred threescore and sixteen souls."
Acts 27:37

"... the assemblies of violent men have sought after my soul."
Psalm 86:14

"For the life of the flesh is in the blood; ... Therefore I said to the children of Israel, No soul of you shall eat blood, ... For it is the life of all flesh; the blood of it is for the life thereof ... ."
Leviticus 17:11-14

III. Soul = Inner Life (the immaterial, invisible part of man)

"Because thou wilt not leave my soul in Hell, neither wilt thou suffer thine Holy One to see corruption."
Acts 2:27

"And he stretched himself upon the child three times,
and cried unto the Lord, and said, O Lord my God,
I pray thee, let this child's soul come into him again.
And the Lord heard the voice of Elijah;
and the soul of the child came into him again, and he revived."
I Kings 17:21,22

"And fear not them which kill the body,
but are not able to kill the soul:
but rather fear Him which is
able to destroy both soul and body in Hell."
Matthew 10:28

IV. Soul = Perceptions, Reflections, Feelings

"... and ye shall find rest unto your souls."
Matthew 11:29

"And Mary said, My soul doth magnify the Lord."
Luke 1:46

"(Yea, a sword shall pierce through thy own soul also,)
that the thoughts of many hearts may be revealed."
Luke 2:35

"Confirming the souls of the disciples,
and exhorting them to continue in the faith ... ."
Acts 14:22

"My soul longeth, yea, even fainteth for the courts of the Lord:
my heart and my flesh crieth out for the living God."
Psalm 84:2

V. Soul = Earthly Desires

"And the fruits that thy soul lusted after are departed from thee, and all things which were dainty and goodly are departed from thee, and thou shalt find them no more at all."
Revelation 18:14

"For He satisfieth the longing soul, and filleth the hungry soul with goodness."
Psalm 107:9

"Men do not despise a thief, if he steal to satisfy his soul when he is hungry."
Proverbs 6:30

VI. Soul = Will and Purpose

"Thou shalt love the Lord thy God with all thy heart, and with all thy soul and with all thy mind."
Matthew 22:37

"And the multitude of them that believed were of one heart and of one soul ... but they had all things common."
Acts 4:32

As you can see, there are many different uses of the word *soul* in Scripture. Therefore, to get the proper interpretation, we must look at it in the context of which it was written.

❖

Test Your Knowledge

*** All answers to the following questions can be found within the pages of <u>this</u> chapter or the Answer Key (at the back of the book).

CHALLENGE YOURSELF: Test your knowledge without referring to the Answer Key

Chapter 5 – Soul – As Used In Scripture

1. The word *Soul* has only one meaning.
   a. True
   b. False

2. What is the Hebrew word translated for *soul*?
   a. Yeshua
   b. Tsaddek
   c. Agape
   d. Nephesh

3. God *satisfies the longing soul* falls under what definition of soul?
   a. Will and Purpose
   b. Inner Life
   c. People or Individuals
   d. Earthly Desires

4. Elijah said, "Let this child's soul come into him again" is a description of:
   a. Earthly Desires
   b. Perceptions, Reflections, Feelings
   c. Physical life
   d. Inner life

5. How many definitions of the word *Soul* are listed in Chapter 5?
   a. 3
   b. 1
   c. 6
   d. 8

6. The Scripture makes reference to dividing the soul and spirit. What chapter and verse listed below is correct?
   a. Hebrews 12:4
   b. Hebrews 4:13
   c. Hebrews 4:12
   d. Hebrews 5:12

7. The scripture, "Thou shalt love the Lord thy God with all thy heart, and with all thy soul and with all thy mind," Matthew 22:37, is listed under The Soul definition VI (Will and Purpose).
   a. True
   b. False

8. The definition listed for Soul *V* is ______________________________.

9. Which of the following definition(s) make reference to the soul.
   a. Physical Life
   b. Perceptions, Reflections, Feelings
   c. Inner Life
   d. All of the above

10. The definition listed for *Soul* in Roman numeral *III* is ______________ ____.

HOW WELL DID YOU DO?

GRADE SCALE

Missed 0 = Excellent
Missed 1 = Very Good
Missed 2 = Good
Missed 3 = Average
Mised 4 or more = Need to Re-read Chapter

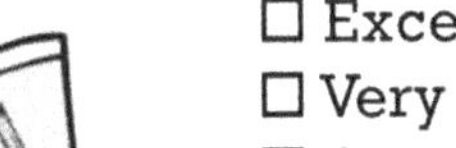

☐ Excellent
☐ Very Good
☐ Good
☐ Average
☐ Need to Re-read Chapter

6

Spirit ~ As Used In Scripture

There is more to the physical body than the visible elements (dust) from which it is made. Adam was created from the dust of the earth and given five senses (sight, touch, taste, hearing, smelling) in which he could use to relate to the earthly environment around him.

The Holy Scriptures show that mankind was given (within the human body) an internal spirit which was formed and placed there by God. In reference to the scriptures below, one of the Hebrew (Old Testament) words translated for "spirit" is *ruwach [rü'·akh]*, and the Greek (New Testament) word is *pneuma [pnyü'-mä]* which can mean either breath, wind, mind, human spirit, or Holy Spirit.

"But there is a spirit in man: and the inspiration of the Almighty gives them understanding."
Job 32:8

"... saith the Lord, which stretcheth forth the heavens, and layeth the foundation of the earth, and formeth the spirit of man within him."
Zechariah 12:1

"And they fell upon their faces, and said, O God, the God of the spirits of all flesh ... ."
Numbers 16:22

"Then shall the dust return to the earth as it was:
and the spirit shall return unto God who gave it."
Ecclesiastes 12:7

The unseen human spirit is what gives mankind the ability to be on a higher thought-plane and separates humans from the rest of the physical creation.

Humans are different from animals and the rest of creation in many ways. Animals do not have the ability to worship, relate, or interface with God in the same way that humans do. What makes mankind different is the *spirit* that dwells within them.

Adam was given a spirit. As a descendant of Adam, we too were given a spirit, which is the part of us that causes us to have a relationship with the unseen, spiritual world; allowing us to have fellowship with God. This fellowship and communication with God is only possible through the spirit. It's through the human spirit that mankind perceives, loves, and worships God. The Word of God tells us that,

"God is a Spirit: and they that worship Him,
must worship Him **in spirit** *and in truth."*
John 4:24

"The Spirit itself beareth witness **with our spirit,**
that we are the children of God."
Romans 8:16

The spirit (in man) is one of the two elements of human life that the scientific community does not understand or connect to human life function. Apart from the Bible, there is no reliable information about the origin or function of the human spirit.

It is the spirit that connects to the soul, which connects to the body, whereby we can relate and communicate with both heaven and earth. The Bible teaches that mankind has three parts - spirit, soul, and body.

"In whose hand is **the soul** *of every living thing,*
and **the breath** *of all mankind."*
Job 12:10

"And the very God of peace sanctify you wholly;
and I pray God your whole spirit and soul and body

be preserved blameless unto the coming of our Lord Jesus Christ."
I Thessalonians 5:23

The Apostle Paul on different occasions talks about an *inside* spiritual person within us. He uses the Greek word *esō* {e'-sō} which means within or the internal inner man.

"For I delight in the law of God after the inward man."
Romans 7:22

"... but though our outward man perish,
yet the inward man *is renewed day by day."*
2 Corinthians 4:16

"That He would grant you ... to be strengthened
with might by His Spirit in the inner man."
Ephesians 3:16

Lets look at a few (different) ways in which "spirit" is used in Scripture.

I. Spirit = Breath or Inner Life

The spirit is the inward, bodiless, invisible part of man.

"... handle Me, and see;
for a spirit hath not flesh and bones, as ye see Me have."
Luke 24:39

"And my spirit *hath rejoiced in God my Savior."*
Luke 1:47

"For what man knoweth the things of a man,
save the spirit of man which is in him?"
I Corinthians 2:11

"And they laughed Him to scorn, knowing that she was dead.
And He put them all out, and took her by the hand,
and called saying, Maid, arise.
And her spirit came again, *and she arose straightway:*
and He commanded to give her meat."
Luke 8:53-55

"And they stoned Stephen, calling upon God, and saying,
Lord Jesus, receive my spirit. And he kneeled down,
and cried with a loud voice, Lord, lay not this sin to their charge.

And when he had said this, he fell asleep."
Acts 7:59,60

"For as the body without the spirit is dead ... ."
James 2:26

"Then shall the dust return to the earth as it was:
and the spirit shall return unto God who gave it."
Ecclesiastes 12:7

As we can clearly see from Scripture, there is a spirit inside of man. The word "spirit" is also used in other ways as well.

II. Spirit = Perceives, Reflects, Feels, Desires

"Watch and pray, that ye enter not into temptation:
the spirit indeed is willing, but the flesh is weak."
Matthew 26:41

"And immediately when Jesus perceived in His spirit that
they also reasoned within themselves, He said unto them,
Why reason these things in your hearts?"
Mark 2:8

"Now while Paul waited for them at Athens,
his spirit was stirred in him,
when he saw the city wholly given to idolatry."
Acts 17:16

"For I verily, as absent in body, but present in spirit,
have judged already ... as though I were present ... ."
I Corinthians 5:3

"With my soul have I desired Thee in the night;
yea, with my spirit within me will I seek Thee early ... ."
Isaiah 26:9

"Thus saith the Lord God; Woe unto the foolish prophets,
that follow their own spirit, and have seen nothing!"
Ezekiel 13:3

"I Daniel was grieved in my spirit in the midst of my body,
and the visions of my head troubled me."
Daniel 7:15

As I have shown, there are many instances of the word "spirit" in Scripture. To get the proper interpretation of the word, we must look at it in the context in which it was written.

In the English language, we also have many words that have more than one meaning. For example, the words duck, spring, pound, and trunk have many different meanings. How the word is used distinguishes its meaning. The Hebrew and Greek language is the same way. Many times, the only way to determine the correct meaning of a word is to look at the context in which it is written.

Knowledge of the human spirit is of major importance if one is to understand the truth about death and the afterlife. To get this part wrong can cause one to miss the whole concept of what the Bible really teaches on the subject of Death and the Afterlife.

Test Your Knowledge

*** All answers to the following questions can be found within the pages of this chapter or the Answer Key (at the back of the book).

CHALLENGE YOURSELF: Test your knowledge without referring to the Answer Key

Chapter 6 – Spirit – As Used In Scripture

1. ___________ do not have the ability to worship, relate, or interface with God in the same way that _____________do.

2. The human spirit is called:
   a. our spirit
   b. inner man
   c. inward man
   d. a, b, and c

3. We don't need to know much about the human spirit to understand the truth about death and the afterlife.
   a. True
   b. False

4. Adam was created from the dust of the earth and given _____________ ______________________ in which he could use to relate to the earthly environment around him.

5. In reference to the usage of the word "spirit" in chapter 6, what is the (Old Testament) Hebrew word for the human spirit?
   a. Ruwach
   b. Nephesh
   c. Tipharah
   d. Pneuma

6. In reference to the usage of the word "spirit" in chapter 6, what is the (New Testament) Greek word for the human spirit?
   a. Ruwach
   b. Nephesh
   c. Tipharah
   d. Pneuma

7. Which of the following definition(s) refer to the human spirit?
   a. Breath
   b. Inward, Bodiless, Invisible
   c. Perceives, Reflects, Feels, Desires
   d. All of the above

8. God's words says, "… but though our ______________________ perish, yet the ____________ is renewed day by day"… which can be found in verse ___ in 2 Corinthians 4.

9. The Apostle Paul uses the Greek word "nomos" which means *within* or *the internal man.*
   a. True
   b. False

10. God's word says, "The Spirit itself beareth witness with the Holy Spirit, that we are the children of God."
    a. True
    b. False

HOW WELL DID YOU DO?

GRADE SCALE

Missed 0 = Excellent
Missed 1 = Very Good
Missed 2 = Good
Missed 3 = Average
Mised 4 or more = Need to Re-read Chapter

☐ Excellent
☐ Very Good
☐ Good
☐ Average
☐ Need to Re-read Chapter

7

Soul-Sleep ~ Truth or Error?

There are many who believe in soul-sleep. Soul-sleep is the belief that when the body dies, the internal spirit/soul also ceases to function and is in a state of unconsciousness.

The supporters of this doctrine of soul sleep only select certain Scriptures, especially Old Testament Scriptures. Even though I believe in the Holy Spirit inspired, inerrant Word of God, it is very clear from Scripture that many prophets and teachers in the Old Testament did not have a complete or clear understanding of what lies beyond death's door. That is why many questions were asked in the Old Testament about death and the afterlife. Job said,

"But man dieth, and wasteth away:
yea, man giveth up the ghost, and where is he?
If a man die, shall he live again?"
Job 14:10,14

The Psalmist also had questions,

"Wilt thou show wonders to the dead?
Shall the dead arise and praise thee? Selah.
Shall thy lovingkindness be declared in the grave?
Or thy faithfulness in destruction?"
Psalm 88:10,11

These questions reveal that centuries ago, there was uncertainty concerning what happens after death. God does not want us to be ignorant about things concerning death and the afterlife.

This is why God said through Paul,

> ***"But I would not have you to be ignorant, brethren, concerning them which are asleep [dead] ... ."***
> ***I Thessalonians 4:13***

Even though Solomon and others in the Old Testament had questions, Jesus who is much wiser and greater than Solomon, came to give us a full understanding of the mystery of death and the afterlife. Jesus said,

> *"The queen of the south ... for she came from the uttermost parts of the earth to hear the wisdom of Solomon; and, behold, a greater than Solomon is here."*
> *Matthew 12:42*

> *"All these things spake Jesus unto the multitudes in parables; and without a parable spake He not unto them: That it might be fulfilled which was spoken by the prophet, saying, I will open My mouth in parables;* ***I will utter things which have been kept secret from the foundation of the world."***
> *Matthew 13:34,35*

To prove the position of soul-sleep, at first glance, there are arguments that may appear to succeed. When certain statements are taken out of context, they do indeed seem to say there is a thing called soul-sleep.

In the previous chapters, we have seen that in the original language (Hebrew/Greek), words vary in meaning depending on the context.

Therefore, we must look at the context of the word that pertains to death in Scripture, to see whether the writer is talking about the grave, the afterlife, the inner self (soul/spirit), or some other meaning.

We must remember that the Word of God does not contradict itself (other portions of Scripture). If there appear to be contradictions, it is because of our lack of knowledge, wisdom, and understanding of what God is saying.

For those difficult passages, we must compare spiritual things with spiritual things (other portions of Scripture) to get the true interpretation of the subject at hand.

"Which things also we speak, not in the words which
man's wisdom teacheth, but which the Holy Ghost teacheth;
comparing spiritual things with spiritual."
I Corinthians 2:13

It is extremely important to proceed with caution when isolating individual Scriptures to prove a point. To rightly divide God's Word, we must also look at the context in which the verse is stated.

For example, the following Scriptures from the book of Ezekiel are used (in error) to prove the doctrine of soul-sleep. It appears that these Scriptures are saying that the soul/spirit loses consciousness at death.

"Behold, all souls are mine; as the soul of the father,
so also the soul of the son is mine: the soul that sinneth, it shall die.
For I have no pleasure in the death of him that dieth,
saith the Lord God: wherefore turn yourselves, and live ye."
Ezekiel 18:4, 32

When looking at the context of this passage, or when reading Ezekiel chapter eighteen in its entirety, it is clear that the entire chapter is not talking about what happens to the internal soul at death. It is teaching us that one person will not die for the sins of another person. It is talking about the physical life of the person.

Here is another Scripture that is (erroneously) used by many to prove the doctrine of Soul-sleep.

"Put not your trust in princes, nor in the son of man,
in whom there is no help. His breath goeth forth,
he returneth to his earth; in that very day his thoughts perish.
Happy is he that hath the God of Jacob for his help,
whose hope is in the Lord his God."
Psalm 146:3-5

The context of these Scriptures does not teach that the dead are unconscious. But they warn against putting trust in human leaders and in men who die. The human princes die and all their plans perish that they had thought or intended to do. Therefore, instead of putting trust in man, we should rather, put our trust in the Lord who shall live and reign forever to accomplish His will.

Here is another Scripture that is (erroneously) used by many to prove the doctrine of soul-sleep.

"For the living know that they shall die: but the dead
know not any thing, neither have they any more a reward;
for the memory of them is forgotten. Also, their love, and their hatred,
and their envy, is now perished; neither have they any more
a portion for ever in any thing that is done under the sun."
Ecclesiastes 9:5,6

The Good News Bible states the verse this way,

"Their loves, their hates, their passions, all died with them.
They will never again take part in anything that happens in this world."
Ecclesiastes 9:6 GNB

In this text of Scripture, Solomon is letting us know that there are no second chances to get it right, after we leave this life.

"Whatsoever thy hand findeth to do, do it with thy might;
for there is no work, nor device, nor knowledge,
nor wisdom, in the grave, whither thou goest."
Ecclesiastes 9:10

We must understand that Solomon is speaking his viewpoint about death with incomplete knowledge of the afterlife. This is why he had questions.

"... And how dieth the wise man? As the fool.
Therefore I hated life; because the work that is wrought under
the sun is grievous unto me: for all is vanity and vexation of spirit."
Ecclesiastes 2:16,17

"Yea, though he live a thousand years twice told,
yet hath he seen no good: do not all go to one place?"
Ecclesiastes 6:6

"Then I beheld all the work of God, that a man cannot
find out the work that is done under the sun: because though
a man labor to seek it out, yet he shall not find it; yea further;
though a wise man think to know it, yet shall he not be able to find it."
Ecclesiastes 8:17

The Good News Bible says it this way,

"Whenever I tried to become wise and learn what goes on in the world, I realized that you could stay awake night and day and never be able to understand what God is doing. However hard you try, you will never find out. Wise men may claim to know, but they don't."
Ecclesiastes 8:16,17 GNB

Out of all the questions Solomon had, the book of Ecclesiastes later concludes with positive assurance about life after death, which agrees with other portions of Scripture.

"... because man goeth to his long home ... Then shall the dust return to the earth as it was: and the spirit shall return unto God who gave it. For God shall bring every work into judgment, with every secret thing, whether it be good, or whether it be evil."
Ecclesiastes 12:5,7,14

The whole of Scripture agrees, man's physical body does return to dust, and there is another home after death.

"For we know that if our earthly house
of this tabernacle were dissolved,
we have a building of God,
an house not made with hands, eternal in the heavens."
2 Corinthians 5:1

The New Living Translation says it this way,

"For we know that when this earthly tent we live in is taken down
(that is, when we die and leave this earthly body),
we will have a house in Heaven, an eternal body
made for us by God Himself and not by human hands."
2 Corinthians 5:1 NLT

God's Word does not agree with the doctrine of Soul-sleep. The Scripture clearly shows, as we shall see in the following chapters, that the dead are in two places at the same time. The body is in the grave and the soul/spirit is someplace else.

Test Your Knowledge

*** All answers to the following questions can be found within the pages of this chapter or the Answer Key (at the back of the book).

CHALLENGE YOURSELF: Test your knowledge without referring to the Answer Key

Chapter 7 – Soul-Sleep ~ Truth or Error?

1. Soul-sleep is the belief that when the body dies, the internal spirit/soul also ceases to function and is in a state of unconsciousness.
   a. True
   b. False

2. The Holy Ghost teaches by ______________ spiritual things with ________________________.

3. Solomon spoke with complete knowledge of death and the afterlife.
   a. True
   b. False

4. God's Word agrees with the doctrine of Soul-sleep.
   a. True
   b. False

5. If there appear to be contradictions concerning God's Word, it is because of our lack of ______________, __________________, and ____________________ of what God is saying.

6. In Ezekiel 18:4, 32 – "Behold, all souls are mine; as the soul of the father, so also the soul of the son is mine: the soul that sinneth, it shall die. For I have no pleasure in the death of him that dieth, saith the Lord God: wherefore turn yourselves and live ye."

   Which of the following statements do not apply to the scriptures above?

   a. It is teaching us that one person will not die for the sins of another person.
   b. It is talking about what happens to the internal soul at death.
   c. It is talking about the physical life of the person.
   d. It is saying that the soul/spirit loses consciousness at death.
   e. b and d

7. Solomon spoke about life after death in Ecclesiastes chapter _____ verses___, ___, ___.

8. Solomon concluded that when you're dead, you're done.

   a. True
   b. False

9. The dead are in two places at the same time.

   a. True
   b. False

10. What scripture in this chapter warns against putting trust in human leaders and in men who die because all their plans perish that they had thought or intended to do?

    a. Ecclesiastes 9:10

    b. 2 Corinthians 5:1

    c. Psalm 146:3-5

    d. Job 14:10, 14

GRADE SCALE

Missed 0 = Excellent
Missed 1 = Very Good
Missed 2 = Good
Missed 3 = Average
Mised 4 or more = Need to Re-read Chapter

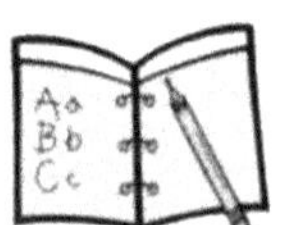

HOW WELL DID YOU DO?

☐ Excellent
☐ Very Good
☐ Good
☐ Average
☐ Need to Re-read Chapter

8

Life After Death

When addressing the subject of life after death, Solomon wrote as things appeared to (who the Bible refers to as) "wise man under the sun." But when Jesus spoke of life after death, He came with wisdom much greater than Solomon and showed us the way things actually are after death.

The Scriptures are filled with references and make it clear that the soul/spirit continues to exist in a conscious state, apart from the body at death. Given to us are many Scriptures that speak of human speech, desires, and admonitions which take place after one dies.

"For He is not a God of the dead, but of the living: for all live unto Him."
Luke 20:38

On the Mount of Transfiguration, two long-dead heroes of Israel - Moses and Elijah, appeared before the disciples and they recognized them.

"And after six days Jesus taketh Peter, James, and John his brother, and bringeth them up into an high mountain apart ... And, behold, there appeared unto them Moses and Elias talking with Him."
Matthew 17:1,3

These patriarchs, Moses and Elijah, though physically dead; are yet alive. Their bodies may have long decayed, but their souls were not asleep, because the soul/spirit never loses consciousness.

When speaking to the Jews about those who believe on Him, Jesus said,

*"Verily, verily, I say unto you, If a man keep My saying,
he shall never see death. Your father Abraham rejoiced
to see My day: and he saw it, and was glad."
John 8:51,56*

As we shall see later (in chapter 15) when we talk about Paradise, Jesus said that "Abraham rejoiced to see My day". Jesus was speaking of when (after His death on the Cross) He would enter into the underworld (Paradise) with the Good News that redemption had now been bought and paid for. Abraham could not have rejoiced if his soul/spirit fell asleep when his body died. Therefore, Abraham (in another state of being) was still alive. In the underground spirit world, Abraham met Christ. Peter said,

*"By which also He [Jesus] went and preached unto the spirits in prison .... "
I Peter 3:19*

The thief on the cross was told on the very day, at the moment of death, he would be with Jesus in Paradise.

*"And Jesus said unto him, Verily I say unto thee,
Today shalt thou be with Me in Paradise."
Luke 23:43*

Those who teach soul sleep say that the translators put the comma in the wrong place. Therefore, suggesting that Jesus did not mean (that very day), but One Day, the thief on the Cross would be with Him in Paradise. That is error, because that theory does not agree with other portions of Scripture.

Eye witnesses confirmed that the physical body of Jesus was dead and in the tomb, while other Scriptures say that (at the same time) His soul/spirit was alive and conscious someplace else.

*"Now that He ascended, what is it but that
He also descended first into the lower parts of the earth?"
Ephesians 4:9*

*"He seeing this before spake of the resurrection of Christ, that
His soul was not left in Hell, neither His flesh did see corruption."
Acts 2:31*

Stephen, a deacon and the first martyr after the ascension of Jesus Christ, believed in a conscious afterlife. When he was about to die from being stoned, he asked the Lord to receive his spirit.

"And they stoned Stephen, calling upon God,
and saying, Lord Jesus, receive my spirit."
Acts 7:59

Paul stated that he desired to be with Christ which was far better than staying on the earth. He would not have made that statement if he knew he would be unconscious in the grave. For how could unconsciousness be "far better" than conscious communion with Jesus Christ in this life? It would have been better for him to remain alive and teach the church.

"For me to live is Christ, and to die is gain.
For I am in a strait betwixt two, having a desire to depart,
and to be with Christ; which is far better."
Philippians 1:21,23

"We are confident, I say, and willing rather
to be absent from the body, and to be present with the Lord."
2 Corinthians 5:8

Jesus said that the soul can survive the death of the body.

"And fear not them which kill the body;
but are not able to kill the soul .... "
Matthew 10:28

Another case of afterlife soul consciousness is seen in the account with the Tribulation martyrs.

"And when he had opened the fifth seal, I saw under the altar
the souls of them that were slain for the Word of God,
and for the testimony which they held:
And they cried with a loud voice, saying,
How long, O Lord, holy and true, dost thou not judge
and avenge our blood on them that dwell on the earth?

And white robes were given unto every one of them;
and it was slain unto them, that they should rest yet for
a little season until their fellow servants also and their
brethren that should be killed as they were, should be fulfilled."
Revelation 6:9-11

In looking at these Scriptures, we see believers who had been killed and are physically dead, yet their souls/spirits are alive in another state and they are conscious and awake. They are able to speak to the Lord and are being spoken to. They are even crying with loud voices for their blood to be avenged for what had been done to them.

In Heaven are found, not only "thousands upon thousands of angels in joyful assembly", but also with them are,

"... the spirits of just men made perfect."
Hebrews 12:23

The statements above teach that the internal soul/spirit of man survives the death of the body, and lives on in consciousness, yet invisible to us. Those that attempt to prove the doctrine of soul sleep will have to deny or explain away all these instances of Scripture that clearly show the dead living in another state, after the physical death of the body.

The thief on the cross, Stephen, Paul, and others looked forward to immediately being with Christ after death and so should we believers. Jesus said,

"For He is not a God of the dead, but of the living:
for all live unto Him."
Luke 20:38

Test Your Knowledge

*** All answers to the following questions can be found within the pages of <u>this</u> chapter or the Answer Key (at the back of the book).

CHALLENGE YOURSELF: Test your knowledge without referring to the Answer Key

Chapter 8 – Life After Death

1. The Scripture teaches that the internal soul/spirit of man survives the death of the body and lives on in consciousness, yet invisible to us.
   a. True
   b. False

2. _______ said, "to die is gain ... and to be with Christ ... is far better."

3. Which Seal was opened and John saw the souls of them under the altar that were slain for the Word of God and for the testimony which they held.
   a. First
   b. Third
   c. Seventh
   d. Fifth

4. What time frame was the thief (on the cross) to be with Jesus in Paradise?
   a. One day
   b. End of the world
   c. That very day
   d. When the trumpet sounds

5. What two patriarchs appeared before Jesus and the disciples on the Mount of Transfiguration?

   a. Moses and Elisha

   b. Elijah and Joshua

   c. Moses and Enoch

   d. Elijah and Moses

6. In the Book of ___________________chapter _____ and verse _____ Jesus says that we should not fear those who are able to kill the body.

7. Those who teach soul-sleep (in error) say that the translators put the ________________ in the wrong place.

8. When Jesus dismissed His Spirit, our redemption (ransom) was immediately paid-in-full, and He immediately ascended on high.

   a. True

   b. False

9. Jesus said, when speaking to the Jews about those who believe on him "… If a man keep ______________, he shall never ________________. Your father Abraham rejoiced to _____________________________: and he _________________, and was glad."

10. Stephen, a deacon and the first martyr after the ascension of Jesus Christ, in Acts 7:59, called upon God saying, "… Lord Jesus, _____________________________________."

HOW WELL DID YOU DO?

GRADE SCALE

Missed 0 = Excellent
Missed 1 = Very Good
Missed 2 = Good
Missed 3 = Average
Mised 4 or more = Need to Re-read Chapter

☐ Excellent
☐ Very Good
☐ Good
☐ Average
☐ Need to Re-read Chapter

9

The Spiritual Underworld

Our thinking and our life on a day-to-day basis is influenced by what we believe. Therefore, the subject of the spiritual underworld is very important to our decision making processes as we walk through this world.

According to Scripture, when the body dies, there is one of two realms or places that the soul/spirit can go, either Heaven or Hell. In Scripture, there are many descriptions of Heaven and there are many descriptions of the underworld called 'Hell'.

Interesting Survey

"There are surveys that indicate a large proportion of people actually believe that the physical world that we live in isn't "all there is" to reality. Many believe in some sort of place of reward for good people after death which they call Heaven; a significant, though relatively smaller, number believe in a place of punishment for evil people which they call Hell.

***Belief in Afterlife** - Monday, April 25, 2011 - **New York** — A poll conducted by global research company Ipsos for Reuters News*

The findings below are from a survey conducted in 23 countries among 18,829 adults.

***The Sweet Hereafter—or Not...** Just over half of global citizens (51%) say they believe in some form of afterlife: one quarter (23%) believe in an afterlife "but not specifically in a heaven or hell", two in ten (19%) believe "you go to heaven or hell", another 7% believe "you are ultimately reincarnated" and 2% believe in "heaven but not hell."*

Alternatively, one quarter (23%) say "you simply cease to exist" whereas another quarter (26%) say they "don't know what happens."

The survey was conducted in 23 countries via the Ipsos Online Panel system.

The subject of Hell is a very hot topic and one that is greatly misunderstood. Views about Hell vary greatly. There are many in this world who try to extinguish the reality of the literal Hell and refuse to accept that such a place exists.

What the Bible says about Hell is mocked by many and does not fit the new age, modern, humanitarian concepts of punishment. Many modern translations of the Bible have even removed the word Hell.

Concerning Hell, there are some who allow their imagination to run wild as they picture a horned-red-devil and demons with pitchforks inflicting many unimaginable types of brutal torture upon their victims; while having a great time ruling the underworld.

This approach is very unscriptural and is found nowhere in the Word of God. Revelation 20:10 makes it plain that the devil himself is among those undergoing punishment, not ruling over an evil empire in Hell.

Although many disagree on details about death and the afterlife, the surveys also indicate that only a very tiny percentage of people have actually read much (or any) of the Bible. So where did they get the details of what they think about death and the afterlife?

We must remember that the truth about Hell can only be found in the Bible. We must place rightly divided Biblical teaching above the ideas of society.

Even though the world tries to extinguish the reality of Hell — they have not destroyed the place, because the Scriptures confirm that Hell is real. Personally, when I was without Jesus Christ in my life (secretly) I carried with me the fear of Hell on the inside. I fooled a lot of friends who thought I had peace of mind. I was able to hide the fact that I was constantly tormented by the thought of one day going to Hell.

Concerning, the word Hell, it is often thought of in many ways. Some say "Hell" burns now below us. Others say "Hell" is in the future (at the end of the world). While others say, "Life is hell."

Some of the greatest *theological confusion* centers around what happens to the soul at the time of physical death and the truth about Hell-Fire. There are many different teachings that attempt to answer these questions.

We must be careful not to be led astray by the teaching of false doctrines. Many erroneous doctrines are used by Satan to deceive, distract, and blind hearts and minds from having a personal relationship with Jesus Christ. Thereby, causing many to fail in properly preparing for eternity.

Two of the major doctrines that are used to deny what the Bible teaches about the reality of Hell are <u>Soul-Sleep</u> and the <u>Annihilation</u> (total destruction) of those who are unbelievers.

Many think that "when you're dead, you're done" to just sleep away throughout all eternity. There are also those who think unbelievers will be completely destroyed, as if nothing ever mattered concerning how they lived in this life. Let's see!

In Holy Scripture, there is a place of punishment in a certain part of God's creation. It is a place called Hell. There is a Hell because the holiness of God demands it.

Because of Satan's rebellion that took place in Heaven, Hell was originally prepared for the devil and his angels, as confirmed according to the Gospel of Matthew,

"... into everlasting fire, prepared for the devil and his angels."
Matthew 25:41

In Scripture, we are given different images under which Hell is represented. It is humanly impossible to comprehend the Bible's description of Hell. Nothing on earth can compare with it. Hollywood cannot produce terror or fright to match the Hell that Jesus spoke of. No crime scene with all its blood and gore could begin to match it's horror. I believe the reality of Hell will infinitely surpass our boldest horrific picture of it.

Many joke about Hell, but Hell is no joke. The Bible continually warns of the place called Hell.

Jesus Christ was the most loving and kindest Man to ever walk the face of the earth. Yet, He took Hell very seriously and warned about it on many occasions. Interestingly, Jesus spoke more on Hell than any other subject.

The whole Bible has much to say about the fate of the lost. There are serious consequences of rejecting God's love and mercy through Jesus Christ. God has gone through great lengths to make sure that none be lost.

"The Lord is ... longsuffering to us-ward, not willing that any should perish, but that all should come to repentance."
2 Peter 3:9

There is a lot left unsaid and unclear about the spiritual underworld of the dead. Many struggle with the fact of someone enduring constant, conscious torment. This should not leave any of us with an unhealthy fear of God. If the thought of some receiving punishment after death is troubling, the solution does not lie in denying the Bible's inspiration, nor in explaining-away Jesus' words by distorting their meaning. We must not attempt to add to the Word of God by trying to fill in the gaps with our logic and intellectual efforts. God has placed in His Word what He wants us to know.

The Lord is good to all. Concerning those who do evil, and their eternal fate – the Judge of all the earth will do that which is right. No one will ever be able to accuse God of being cruel, unfair, or unloving.

Hell As Used In The Bible

The word "Hell" is used 54 times in the King James Version of the Bible. We must keep in mind that there were more words in the Hebrew (Old Testament) and Greek (New Testament) language to represent *Hell* than there were in the English language. Therefore, the word *Hell* does not mean the same thing in every verse where it is found in Scripture.

To think that *Hell* means the same thing in every verse where it is found, has caused much confusion among many. It takes rightly dividing the Word of Truth to show forth the different usages of these words. This is why the Scripture commands us to,

"Study to shew thyself approved unto God,
a workman that needeth not to be ashamed,
rightly dividing the Word of Truth."
2 Timothy 2:15

Let's look at the meaning of each of these words and see what the Bible teaches about each one as it talks about Hell.

- The Grave - *qeber* [keh'·ver]
- Sheol - *shĕ'owl* [sheh·ōle']
- Hades - *hadēs* [hä'-dās]
- Tartaroo - *tartaroō* [tär-tä-ro'-ō]
- Gehenna - *geenna* [ge'-en-nä]
- Paradise - *paradeisos* [pä-rä'-dā-sos]
- Lake of Fire
- The Second Death

❖

Test Your Knowledge

*** All answers to the following questions can be found within the pages of this chapter or the Answer Key (at the back of the book).

CHALLENGE YOURSELF: Test your knowledge without referring to the Answer Key

Chapter 9 – The Spiritual Underworld

1. Originally, Hell was prepared for ______________________ and ___________________.

2. No one will ever be able to accuse God of being __________, __________, or ___________.

3. How many times is the word Hell seen in Scripture in the King James Version of the Bible?
   a. 21
   b. 31
   c. 54
   d. 34

4. Many modern translations of the Bible have removed the word Hell.
   a. True
   b. False

5. According to the Ipsos Online Panel Survey on April 25, 2011 from 23 countries among 18, 829 people, what percentage believe in Heaven but not Hell?
   a. 2%
   b. 51%
   c. 26%
   d. 23%

6. According to the Ipsos Online Panel Survey on April 25, 2011 from 23 countries among 18, 829 people, when asked about their belief in Heaven and Hell, 26 % responded by saying which of the following?
   a. You are ultimately reincarnated
   b. You go to Heaven or Hell
   c. You simply cease to exist
   d. Don't know what happens

7. Revelation 20:10 makes it plain that ________________ is among those undergoing punishment, and not ________ over an _________ ______________ in Hell.

8. What are two of the major doctrines that are used to deny what the Bible teaches about the reality of Hell?
   a. The Trinity
   b. Soul-Sleep
   c. Death, Burial, and the Resurrection
   d. Annihilation

9. The word *Hell* is an English word that translators of the English Bible used to express the sense of the Hebrew word ____________ and the Greek words _____________, ___________, and ____________.

10. In the Bible, scriptures concerning Hell have different terms or meanings referencing to Hell. Which of the following is not an accurate reference to the word Hell?

    a. The Grave

    b. Lake of Fire

    c. Tipharah

    d. Tartaroo

    e. The Second Death

    f. Sheol

    g. Soul-Sleep

    h. Paradise

    i. Gehenna

    j. Hades

HOW WELL DID YOU DO?

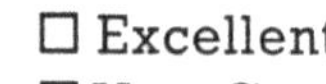

GRADE SCALE

Missed 0 = Excellent
Missed 1 = Very Good
Missed 2 = Good
Missed 3 = Average
Mised 4 or more = Need to Re-read Chapter

☐ Excellent
☐ Very Good
☐ Good
☐ Average
☐ Need to Re-read Chapter

10

The Grave

The grave is a place where the physical remains of those who have died are deposited. It can be a hole in the ground, a cave, a specially prepared vault, or any place used to lay dead bodies to rest.

When the biblical authors spoke of the grave, they used the Hebrew word *qeber [keh'·ver]* which is the most common word for grave, or a burial place.

Strongs Exhaustive Concordance of the Bible #6913 says, Qeber= a sepulcher, burying place, grave.

Two other words that are used for a burial place in the Old Testament are *Shachath [shakh'·ath]* and *Qbuwrah [keb-oo-raw']*.

"And they said unto Moses, Because there were no graves [qebers] in Egypt, hast thou taken us away to die in the wilderness? ... ."
Exodus 14:11

"Yet shall he be brought to the grave [qeber], and shall remain in the tomb."
Job 21:32

"... my days are extinct, the graves [qebers] are ready for me."
Job 17:1

"... who slew him with the sword, and cast his dead body into the graves [qebers], of the common people."
Jeremiah 26:23

Qeber (grave) is a place where the physical body suffers destruction through the corruption of decay. The grave is a place of corruption, whereby the body returns to dust. There is no consciousness of life in the grave. God said to Adam,

"... for dust thou art, and unto dust shalt thou return."
Genesis 3:19

The prophet Ezekiel was set down in midst of a graveyard (qeber). There was no life there, which is evident when Ezekiel said,

"The hand of the Lord was upon me, and carried me out in the spirit of the Lord, and set me down in the midst of the valley which was full of bones."
Ezekiel 37:1

When the Bible speaks of corruption, it is talking about the destruction and decay of the body. When speaking of the physical body of Jesus, the Scripture says,

"That He should still live for ever, and not see corruption."
Psalm 49:9

"... neither wilt Thou suffer Thine Holy One [Jesus] to see corruption."
Psalm 16:10

As we seek to understand what the Bible really teaches about death and the afterlife, we must constantly be aware of the difference between Qeber (grave) and Sheol (Hell). They are not the same.

- Qeber [grave] is the fate of the body.
- Sheol [Hell] is the fate of the spirit/soul.

They are always contrasted and never equal.

❖

Test Your Knowledge

*** All answers to the following questions can be found within the pages of this chapter or the Answer Key (at the back of the book).

CHALLENGE YOURSELF: Test your knowledge without referring to the Answer Key

Chapter 10 – The Grave

1. Which Hebrew word does not refer to the Grave?
   a. Shachath
   b. Qbuwrah
   c. Mnema
   d. Qeber

2. There is no difference between the Grave and Hell.
   a. True
   b. False

3. In the Old Testament, the Hebrew word __________ is the fate of the spirit/soul.

4. In the Old Testament, the Hebrew word __________ is the fate of the body.

5. When the Bible speaks of corruption it is not talking about the destruction and decay of the body but the immortality of the body.
   a. True
   b. False

6. Circle the following places which are considered a Grave?
   a. Sepulcher
   b. Vault
   c. Cave
   d. Hole in the ground
   e. All of the above

7. When Jesus died on the cross, the Word says, His body did see corruption.
   a. True
   b. False

8. Qeber and Sheol are always __________________ and never __________________.

9. In Genesis 3:19, Joshua said, "… for dust thou art, and unto dust shalt thou return."
   a. True
   b. False

10. Which Hebrew word is the most *common* word for Grave?

    a. Shachath

    b. Qbuwrah

    c. Mnema

    d. Qeber

HOW WELL DID YOU DO?

GRADE SCALE

Missed 0 = Excellent
Missed 1 = Very Good
Missed 2 = Good
Missed 3 = Average
Mised 4 or more = Need to Re-read Chapter

☐ Excellent
☐ Very Good
☐ Good
☐ Average
☐ Need to Re-read Chapter

11

Hell = Sheol

The word *Sheol - shĕ'owl [sheh·ōle']* is found in the Hebrew text of the Old Testament 65 times. Sheol is translated in the King James Version as - "Hell" 31 times, "the Pit" 3 times, and "the Grave" 31 times.

Because Sheol is at times translated *Hell* and other times translated as *Grave*, there has been much misunderstanding - causing many to teach that Sheol means the grave. We have already seen that the word [qeber] is the word used for a physical grave where dead bodies are laid to rest.

Sheol is a place described in the Old Testament as the *nether* or *underworld* - the abode of the dead. God never put forth the concept of annihilation or nonexistence as the fate of man's soul/spirit at death.

A careful examination of Old Testament Scripture shows that a person does not cease to exist at death. But the Bible consistently shows that the grave [qeber] claims the physical part of man (the body) and Sheol [Hell] claims the separated, spiritual part of man (the soul).

Sheol in the Old Testament was a temporary place where conscious, disembodied (departed) souls/spirits of the dead were kept.

"... her guests are in the depths of Hell [Sheol]."
Proverbs 9:18

Sheol (Hell) is under the earth, while *graves* were built as sepulchers and tombs above the earth, in man-made caves or holes in the earth.

Sheol does not refer to the grave or to passing into nonexistence. When the body dies, a person's soul/spirit enters a new kind of existence and experience. In Sheol, the person's soul/spirit continues to be aware of what is going on around them and is capable of memory, speech, recognition, and communication, without the need of a physical body. This can be proven in scripture.

The first mention of Sheol in the Old Testament is found in Genesis.

"And all his sons and all his daughters rose up to comfort him;
but he refused to be comforted; and he said,
For I will go down into the grave [Sheol] unto my son mourning. ... ."
Genesis 37:35

The Jerusalem Bible translates this verse as follows,

"All his sons and daughters came to comfort him, but he refused to be comforted. 'No,' he said 'I will go down in mourning to Sheol, beside my son' ... ."
Genesis 37:35 TJB

While death meant separation from the living, the Old Testament saints clearly understood that it also meant reunion with the departed. The Old Testament saints looked forward to reuniting with their departed loved ones. This is why over and over again (in the Scriptures) we see the term "gathered unto his people." This means reuniting with the souls of those who have died, in the place of departed spirits.

God said to Abraham,

"And thou shalt go to thy fathers in peace [Sheol];
thou shalt be buried [qeber] in a good old age."
Genesis 15:15

"Then Abraham gave up the ghost, and died in a good old age,
an old man, and full of years; and was gathered to his people [Sheol]."
Genesis 25:8

"And Isaac gave up the ghost, and died, and was
gathered unto his people [Sheol], being old and full of days:
and his sons Esau and Jacob buried [qeber] him."
Genesis 35:29

"And when Jacob had made an end of commanding his son,
he gathered up his feet into the bed, and yielded up the ghost,
and was gathered unto his people [Sheol]."
Genesis 49:33

"And die in the mount whither thou goest up, and be
gathered unto thy people; as Aaron thy brother died in mount Hor,
and was gathered unto his people."
Deuteronomy 32:50

"So Moses the servant of the Lord died there in the land of Moab,
according to the word of the Lord. And he buried [qeber] him
in a valley in the land of Moab, over against Beth-peor:
but no man knoweth of his sepulcher [qeber] unto this day."
Deuteronomy 34:5,6

David also believed in consciousness after death, because when his newborn son died, he said,

"But now he is dead, wherefore should I fast?
Can I bring him back again?
I shall go to him [Sheol], but he shall not return to me."
2 Samuel 12:23

In the Old Testament Scriptures, we have a Hebrew word called *rapha' [rä·fä']*. Strongs Exhaustive Concordance - H7496 says, *[rapha]* means the dead (ghosts of the dead, shades, spirits).

"For her house inclineth unto death, and her paths unto the dead [rapha]."
Proverbs 2:18

"But he knoweth not that the dead are there;
and that her guests [rapha] are in the depths of Hell [Sheol]."
Proverbs 9:18

King of Babylon and the Underworld

In the book of Isaiah, we have a very interesting passage of Scripture that gives us a little insight into the underworld. God commanded Isaiah to proclaim this proverb against the king of Babylon. Whether this is future or has already come to pass, is not known.

God says through the prophet, tell the proud king of Babylon that conquered many and ruled with a cruel hand, that he is about to die. His earthly possessions and his status as king of Babylon will mean nothing below. The pleasant music he enjoyed and earthly power he enjoyed will all be gone. He will be conscious, helpless, and hopeless as he is taunted in the underworld by the welcoming committee of other departed spirits [rapha]. As a matter of fact (on the earth) his body will not even get a decent burial.

This passage shows conscious communication that takes place in Sheol and this lets us know that it's talking about something other than a burial [qeber] place.

"Hell from beneath is moved for thee to meet thee at thy coming: it stirreth up the dead [rapha] for thee, even all the chief ones of the earth; it hath raised up from their thrones all the kings of the nations.

All they shall speak and say unto thee, Art thou also become weak as we? art thou become like unto us? Thy pomp is brought down to the grave [Sheol], and the noise of thy viols: the worm is spread under thee, and the worms cover thee."
Isaiah 14:9-11

"They that see thee shall narrowly look upon thee, and consider thee, saying, Is this the man that made the earth to tremble, that did shake kingdoms; That made the world as a wilderness, and destroyed the cities thereof; that opened not the house of his prisoners?

All the kings of the nations, even all of them, lie in glory, every one in his own house. But thou art cast out of thy grave [qeber] like an abominable branch, and as the raiment of those that are slain, thrust through with a sword, that go down to the stones of the pit; as a carcase trodden under feet. Thou shalt not be joined with them in burial [qeber], because thou hast destroyed thy land, and slain thy people: the seed of evildoers shall never be renowned."
Isaiah 14:16-20

The Jerusalem Bible quotes this same passage as follows,

"On your account Sheol beneath us is astir to greet your arrival.
To honor you he rouses the ghosts [rapha] of all the rulers of the world.
He makes all the kings of the nation get up from their thrones.

Each has something to say and what they will say to you is this,
'So you too have been brought to nothing, like ourselves.

You, too, have become like us. Your magnificence has been flung down to Sheol with the music of your harps; underneath you a bed of maggots, and over you a blanket of worms."
Isaiah 14:9-11 (TJB)

"What! Now you have fallen to Sheol to the very bottom of the abyss! All who see you will gaze at you, will stare at you, 'Is this the man who made the earth tremble, and overthrew kingdoms, who made the world a desert and leveled cities, who never to his captives opened the prison gates?'

All the kings of the nations lie honorably, each in his tomb. But you, you have been expelled from your grave [qeber] like loathsome dung, buried under the slaughtered, under those cut down by the sword, and thrown on the stones of the ditch like a mangled carcase. You are never going to rejoin them in the grave [qeber], for you have brought your country to ruin and destroyed your people."
Isaiah 14:16-20 (TJB)

Sheol cannot be the grave *here* because the body and soul are in different places. The soul is in Sheol with other departed souls, while the body remains unburied, or outside of the grave to be infested by maggots.

In the text of Isaiah 14:12-15 (not listed), this is a passage commonly used in reference to the downfall of Satan. No doubt, Satan was behind the cruel actions of this Gentile king of Babylon. Regardless, it does not change the fact that Sheol and the grave are in different places.

Kings of Assyria and Egypt and the Underworld

To further prove the point that there is consciousness in the underworld - we also find another similar situation in Ezekiel about the fall of the two mighty kings (of Assyria and Egypt) who ended up in the underworld with those who have gone before them. We should take note that in Ezekiel chapter 31, it was pointed out to Pharaoh that just as the king of Assyria, who was greater than he was, had died and gone into the underworld; so would he.

"Son of man, speak unto Pharaoh king of Egypt, and to his multitude...Therefore thus saith the Lord God; Because thou hast lifted up thyself in height ... I have driven him out for his wickedness.

... for they are all delivered unto death, to the nether parts of the earth, in the midst of the children of men, with them that go down to the Pit ... when I cast him down to Hell [Sheol] with them that descend into the Pit ... ."
Ezekiel 31:2,10,11,14,16

Then we see Pharaoh, the mighty king of Egypt and his host, who had thought themselves invincible because of their strength and fame among the nations, as they too arrive in Sheol. It is pointed out that now, they were just like the great nations who had gone before them. Their individual souls/spirits were confined to Sheol while their bodies decayed in the grave [qeber].

"Son of man, wail for the multitude of Egypt, and cast them down, even her, and the daughters of the famous nations, unto the nether parts [regions underground] of the earth, with them that go down into the Pit."
Ezekiel 32:18

"Whom dost thou pass in beauty? go down, and be thou laid with the uncircumcised. They shall fall in the midst of them that are slain by the sword: she is delivered to the sword: draw her and all her multitudes. The strong among the mighty shall speak to him out of the midst of Hell [Sheol] with them that help him: they are gone down, they lie uncircumcised, slain by the sword."
Ezekiel 32:19-21

"There is Elam and all her multitude round about her grave [qeber], all of the slain, fallen by the sword, which are gone down uncircumcised into the nether parts [regions underground] of the earth, which caused their terror in the land of the living; yet have they borne their shame with them that go down to the Pit."
Ezekiel 32:24

"And they shall lie with the mighty that are fallen of the uncircumcised, which are gone down to Hell [Sheol] with their weapons of war: and they have laid their swords under their heads, but their iniquities shall be upon their bones, though they were the terror of the mighty in the land of the living."
Ezekiel 32:27

These Old Testament Scriptures clearly show that the physical body and the soul/spirit are in two different places. Make no mistake about it, the Old Testament teaches that there is conscious existence of soul/spirit after death.

Test Your Knowledge

*** All answers to the following questions can be found within the pages of this chapter or the Answer Key (at the back of the book).

CHALLENGE YOURSELF: Test your knowledge without referring to the Answer Key

Chapter 11 - Hell = Sheol

1. How many times is Sheol found in the Hebrew text of the Old Testament, King James Version?
   a. 31
   b. 54
   c. 65
   d. 61

2. The Scriptures show that when a person dies their spirit/soul continues to be aware of what is going on around them and is capable of ___________, ___________, _______________, and _______________.

3. After death … what great king was greeted and taunted by those in the underworld as now being as weak, helpless, and hopeless as they were?
   a. Babylon
   b. Sodom
   c. Assyria
   d. Egypt

4. The Hebrew word _________ means the dead (ghosts of the dead, shades, spirits).

5. Sheol is a place described in the Old Testament as the ____________ or ____________ - the __________ of the dead.

6. Sheol in the Old Testament was a __________________________ ________________where________________, ___________________ souls/spirits of the dead were kept.

7. In Scripture, the term "gathered unto his people" made reference to,
   a. Being buried with other family members
   b. Old Testament saints reuniting with departed love one's (spirits)
   c. Both a and b
   d. None of the above

8. The Bible consistently shows in the Old Testament that the Grave [qeber] claims the physical part of man (the body), and Sheol [Hell] claims the separated, spiritual part of man (the soul).

   Which of the following scriptures (in this chapter) clearly communicate the separation of the spirit and the body?

   a. Isaiah 55:1
   b. Ezekiel 1:20
   c. Genesis 15:15
   d. Genesis 35:29

9. Which Hebrew word applies to the spirits of the dead in the Old Testament?
   a. Rapha
   b. Qeber
   c. Sheol
   d. Kuma

10. In this chapter, according to Scripture, of the two mighty kings (Assyria and Egypt) which king went to Sheol, and which king went to the Pit?
    a. King of Assyria went to Sheol, King of Egypt went to the Hades
    b. King of Egypt went to Sheol, King of Assyria went to Gehenna
    c. Both Kings (Assyria and Egypt) went to the Pit/Sheol
    d. None of the above

GRADE SCALE

Missed 0 = Excellent
Missed 1 = Very Good
Missed 2 = Good
Missed 3 = Average
Mised 4 or more = Need to Re-read Chapter

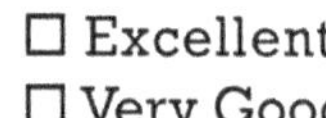

☐ Excellent
☐ Very Good
☐ Good
☐ Average
☐ Need to Re-read Chapter

12

Hell = Hades

H*adēs [hä'-dās]* is the Greek word for *Hell* and is a key term to the Biblical understanding of death and the afterlife. Hades is the bridge that takes us from the Old Testament view of death to the New Testament position.

Hades is the New Testament equivalent of the Old Testament word Sheol. Both of these words speak of the same place. The Apostle Peter clearly shows that Sheol and Hades are the same as he talks about the Lord Jesus Christ and His resurrection. Peter made direct application of this concept as he quoted from the book of Psalms which spoke of Christ's death, burial and resurrection.

"Therefore my heart is glad, and my glory rejoiceth: my flesh also shall rest in hope. For thou wilt not leave my soul in Hell [Sheol]; neither wilt thou suffer thine Holy One to see corruption [qeber or grave]."
Psalm 16:9,10

"He seeing this before spake of the resurrection of Christ, that His soul was not left in Hell [Hades], neither His flesh did see corruption [body left to rot in the grave]."
Acts 2:31

Notice that Peter used Hades for the Old Testament word Sheol to signify what happened to Jesus Christ in the New Testament. Peter uses Hades in the place of Sheol to show that they are identical in meaning.

Thayer's Greek-English Lexicon (p. 11) states that Hades comes from two words which joined together mean *invisible* or *unseen*. Thus it refers to *the common receptacle of disembodied spirits.*

Hades is also defined as "the region of departed spirits of the lost" (but including the blessed dead in periods preceding the ascension of Christ).

Hades is used 11 times in the Greek New Testament, being rendered "Hell" 10 times and "grave" 1 time.

Because Hades is used once in the New Testament as the grave, there has been some misunderstanding determining the difference between Hell and the grave in the folllowing scripture.

"O death, where is thy sting?
O grave [Hades], where is thy victory?"
I Corinthians 15:55

Some have mistakenly taught that Hades always refer to the grave rather than a physical Hell. This erroneous teaching leads to the denial of the existence of an immediate or present Hell and to other false doctrines such as soul-sleep or the unconscious state of the dead. Not once does Hades mean nonexistence or unconsciousness.

Hades Is Not The Grave

Hades is not the grave, because in the New Testament we find three Greek words that refer to the grave, *taphos, mnema,* and *mnemeion.*

1. *Taphos* - [tä'-fos] is used 7 times and is translated "sepulcher" 6 of those times and "tomb" 1 time.
2. *Mnēma* - is used 7 times, being rendered "tomb" 2 times, "grave" 1 time, and "sepulcher" 4 times.
3. *Mnēmeion* - [mnā-mā'-on] is the most common word for grave in the New Testament. It is used 42 times. It is used 5 times as "tomb," 29 times as "sepulcher," and 8 times as "grave."

The grave is a place where the physical body is laid at death. It is a place of corruption whereby the body returns to dust. There is no consciousness of life in the grave, because the soul/spirit which produces physical consciousness has departed. There is only silence in the grave.

Hades Is Not Death

Hades does not mean death, because the Greek word *thanatos* is the word for *death* of the physical body in the New Testament.

Strongs #2288 - *thanatos [thä'-nä-tos]* = the physical death of the body.

Hades is not death because Hades and death are linked together in many passages and are talking about two different things. Jesus said,

"I Am He that liveth, and was dead [thanatos];
and, behold, I am alive for evermore, Amen;
and have the keys of Hell [Hades] and death [thanatos]."
Revelation 1:18

In these few passages, we see a general distinction between the "outward man" which is the body, and the "inward man" which is the soul.

Death or the grave claims the physical part of man - the body.

"... but though our outward man [body] perish .... ."
2 Corinthians 4:16

Hades claims the separated, spiritual part of man - the soul/spirit. Jesus said,

"For as Jonas was three days and three nights in the whale's belly; so shall the Son of Man be three days and three nights in the heart of the earth."
Matthew 12:40

Jesus was letting us know that He would spend the time between His death and resurrection in Hades (the heart of the earth). The body of Jesus rested in the tomb (sepulcher), but His soul/spirit was in a different place (in the heart of the earth). Paul affirms this by saying,

"... what is it but that He also
descended first into the lower parts of the earth?"
Ephesians 4:9

The Apostle Peter writes,

"By which also He went and preached unto the spirits
[pneuma - human soul/spirits that have left the body] in prison."
I Peter 3:19

Apostle Peter spoke of the death of Christ's physical body, and His return from Hades.

> *"Therefore did my heart rejoice, and my tongue was glad;*
> *moreover also my flesh shall rest in hope:*
> *Because thou wilt not leave my soul in Hell [Hades],*
> *neither wilt thou suffer thine Holy One*
> *to see corruption [the decay of the body after death]."*
> *Acts 2:26,27*

Through the life of Christ, we can clearly see that the soul/spirit of man lives on after physical death and remains in a conscious state of being.

Test Your Knowledge

*** All answers to the following questions can be found within the pages of this chapter or the Answer Key (at the back of the book).

CHALLENGE YOURSELF: Test your knowledge without referring to the Answer Key

Chapter 12 – Hell = Hades

1. The New Testament equivalent of the Old Testament Sheol is ________.

2. How many times is the Greek Word *Hades* used in the New Testament?
   a. 7
   b. 9
   c. 16
   d. 11

3. Hades and the grave is the same place.
   a. True
   b. False

4. The Greek word ______________ is the word for *death* of the physical body in the New Testament.

5. Jesus was in the ________ of the earth for ________ days and _______ nights.

6. The body of Jesus rested in the tomb (sepulcher), but His soul/spirit was in a different place (in the heart of the earth).

   a. True

   b. False

7. Which Greek word (New Testament) does not refer to the grave?

   a. Taphos

   b. Qeber

   c. Mnema

   d. Mnemeion

8. What is the most common word used for Grave in the New Testament?

   a. Taphos

   b. Qeber

   c. Mnema

   d. Mnemeion

9. Hades claims the ______________________, ____________________ part of man – the ________.

10. There is no _____________________ of life in the grave, because the soul/spirit which produces ___________________________________ has departed.

HOW WELL DID YOU DO?

GRADE SCALE

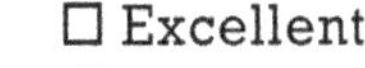

Missed 0 = Excellent
Missed 1 = Very Good
Missed 2 = Good
Missed 3 = Average
Mised 4 or more = Need to Re-read Chapter

☐ Excellent
☐ Very Good
☐ Good
☐ Average
☐ Need to Re-read Chapter

~ 13 ~

Hell = Tartaroo

The Greek word - *tartaroo [tär-tă-ro'-ō]* occurs but once in Scripture and is translated Hell.

"For if God spared not the angels that sinned, but cast them down to Hell [Tartaroo], and delivered them into chains of darkness [gloomy dungeons], to be reserved unto judgment ... ."
2 Peter 2:4

The words *cast down to Hell* are translated from the one Greek word *tartaroo.* The word *tartaroo* very closely resembles *tartarus [tahr-ter-uhs],* a word used in Grecian mythology as the name for a dark abyss or prison [holding compartment] of punishment for the most wicked.

Tartaroo applies to a specific compartment or place of confinement in the underworld [Hades] where a certain class of fallen angels are being held until the time of their judgment.

Not much is said about this evil angelic event, but Jude spoke of an unexplainable phenomenon, whereby a certain group of angels committed a particular wicked crime which caused them to be confined.

"And the angels which kept not their first estate [positions of authority], but left their own habitation, He hath reserved in everlasting chains under darkness unto the judgment of the great day."
Jude 1:6

In Jude verse 5, he is asking the believers to remember this angelic event, and he links it with two other events. The events that Jude links it with are, the unbelief after the exodus, and Sodom and Gomorrah.

It is also interesting to note that Peter links the *angelic* incident, referred to above, with the same time frame.

"And spared not the old world, but saved Noah the eighth person, a preacher of righteousness, bringing in the flood upon the world of the ungodly. And turning the cities of Sodom and Gomorrha into ashes condemned them with an overthrow, making them an example unto those that after should live ungodly."
2 Peter 2:5,6

All of these events speak of wicked, shameless conduct by angels, suggesting that angels slept with natural women and produced giants. There is no other angelic event in Scripture that fits this scenario other than the one in Genesis.

"There were giants in the earth in those days; and also after that, when the sons of God came in unto the daughters of men, and they bare children to them, the same became mighty men which were of old, men of renown."
Genesis 6:4

The term *sons of God* refers to angelic beings.

"Now there was a day when the sons of God came to present themselves before the LORD, and Satan came also among them."
Job 1:6

"Again there was a day when the sons of God came to present themselves before the LORD, and Satan came also among them to present himself before the LORD."
Job 2:1

Somehow, it seems that certain fallen angels caused a disruption of normal genetic patterns, and were confined to Hell [Tartaroo].

Presently, this is all that God has chosen to reveal concerning this wicked angelic event. In the future, if God chooses to open our understanding of this event, we'll have a clear picture of what actually happened to cause this angelic confinement.

❖

Test Your Knowledge

*** All answers to the following questions can be found within the pages of this chapter or the Answer Key (at the back of the book).

CHALLENGE YOURSELF: Test your knowledge without referring to the Answer Key

Chapter 13 – Hell = Tartaroo

1. In Genesis 6:4, the term *sons of God* refers to ___________________.

2. Certain fallen angels were confined to which section of Hell?

   a. Gehenna

   b. Paradise

   c. Tartaroo

   d. Sheol

3. What two cities are an example to those who live ungodly?

   ______________ and _______________.

4. Jude spoke of an unexplainable phenomenon, a certain group of angels who committed a particular wicked crime. In Jude, he asks the believers to remember this angelic event and links it with two other events. What are the two events?

   a. The unbelief after the Exodus

   b. The Flood

   c. Burning Sodom and Gomorrah into ashes

   d. a, c

5. The angels that kept not their first estate, what is their state:
   a. Roaming free
   b. Tormenting people in the Underworld
   c. In everlasting chains
   d. Having a good time with the devil in Hell

6. Tartaroo applies to a ____________________ or _______________ in the underworld [Hades] where a certain class of _______________ are being held until the time of their ____________________.

7. The Greek word Tartaroo [Hell] is referred in Scripture at least eight times in the New Testament.
   a. True
   b. False

8. In Genesis, chapter _____ and verse ____ talks about the fallen angels which caused a disruption of normal genetic patterns.

9. Job, chapter 1, verse ____ also makes reference to *the sons of God.*

10. The words *cast down to Hell* are translated from the one Greek word Tartaroo.
    a. True
    b. False

11. Which of the following is NOT a description of Tartarus, a word used in Grecian mythology which closely resembles Tartaroo?

    a. Place of punishment for the most wicked

    b. A dark abyss

    c. A prison

    d. None of the above

HOW WELL DID YOU DO?

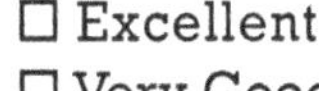

GRADE SCALE

Missed 0 = Excellent
Missed 1 = Very Good
Missed 2 = Good
Missed 3 = Average
Mised 4 or more = Need to Re-read Chapter

☐ Excellent
☐ Very Good
☐ Good
☐ Average
☐ Need to Re-read Chapter

14

Hell = Gehenna

The word *Gehenna [ge'-en-nä]* is found 12 times in the Greek New Testament. "Gehenna," which is derived from the Hebrew word hinnom - means "a place of burning." The "Valley of Hinnom," which translated into Greek becomes Gehenna.

The word Gehenna was originally referred to as the Valley of Hinnom, which was just outside the city of Jerusalem. In the Old Testament, it was the place where idolatrous Jews gave human sacrifices to pagan gods.

"Ahaz ... he did not that which was right in the sight of the Lord. Moreover he burnt incense in the valley of the son of Hinnom, and burnt his children in the fire, after the abominations of the heathen whom the LORD had cast out before the children of Israel."
2 Chronicles 28:1,3

Because of these horrible idolatrous practices, the Valley of Hinnom was hated and considered *unclean* by pious Jews.

In Christ's day, this hatred of the Valley of Hinnom caused it to become the dump and garbage burner to the city for the burning of refuse. The fire continually burned and they cast into it all kinds of filth, together with the carcasses of beasts, and the unburied bodies of criminals who had been executed. With many remaining relics/corpses that were around, the worms were always feeding. Because of this, the Valley of Hinnom became a graphic symbol of the place of punishment for the wicked.

Out of its 12 occurrences in the New Testament, 11 of those times Gehenna was mentioned by Jesus. Jesus deliberately used the word Gehenna to impress upon His hearers that eternal punishment, as a consequence of sin, awaits the wicked after the resurrection.

The scriptures listed below are serious warnings from Jesus about the terrible reality of God's judgment in the world to come. Jesus says,

"... but whosoever shall say, Thou fool,
shall be in danger of Hell [Gehenna] fire."
Matthew 5:22

"And if thy right eye offend thee, pluck it out, and cast it from thee:
for it is profitable for thee that one of thy members should perish, and not
that thy whole body should be cast into Hell [Gehenna]."
Matthew 5:29

"And if thy right hand offend thee, cut it off, and cast it from thee:
for it is profitable for thee that one of thy members should perish,
and not that thy whole body should be cast into Hell [Gehenna]."
Mattthew 5:30

"And fear not them which kill the body, but are not
able to kill the soul: but rather fear him which is able
to destroy both soul and body in Hell [Gehenna]."
Matthew 10:28

"And if thine eye offend thee, pluck it out, and cast it from thee:
it is better for thee to enter into life with one eye,
rather than having two eyes to be cast into Hell [Gehenna] fire."
Matthew 18:9

"Woe unto you, scribes and Pharisees, hypocrites! for ye compass
sea and land to make one proselyte, and when he is made,
ye make him twofold more the child of Hell [Gehenna] than yourselves."
Matthew 23:15

"Ye serpents, ye generation of vipers,
how can ye escape the damnation of Hell [Gehenna]?"
Matthew 23:33

"And if thy foot offend thee, cut it off: it is better for thee
to enter halt into life, than having two feet to be cast
into Hell [Gehenna], into the fire that never shall be quenched:

Where their worm dieth not, and the fire is not quenched."
Mark 9:45,46

"But I will forewarn you Whom ye shall fear:
Fear Him, which after He hath killed hath power
to cast into Hell [Gehenna]; yea, I say unto you, Fear Him."
Luke 12:5

Gehenna, as Biblically described, is a permanent, eternal place of punishment in which the unfaithful and wicked reside forever. Gehenna is not to be confused with Hades or Sheol. They are different places.

While Sheol and Hades describe the temporary abode of the dead until the resurrection, Gehenna is the place of future punishment of the unrepentant angels and unbelievers for all eternity.

From looking at the Scriptural expressions that describe the eternal state of the wicked as being forever separated from God, it seems that Gehenna, the Lake of Fire, and the Second Death are identical terms.

"And death [thanatos] and Hell [Hades] were cast
into the Lake of Fire [Gehenna]. This is the Second Death."
Revelation 20:14

Gehenna is the place where the body as well as the soul is punished. Jesus said,

"And fear not them which kill the body, but are not able to
kill the soul: but rather fear Him which is able to
destroy both soul and body in Hell [Gehenna]."
Matthew 10:28

The word *destroy* comes from the Greek word *apollumi [ä-po'l-lü-mē]* = which means *to be delivered up to eternal misery.*

The wicked that are cast into Gehenna do not get annihilated, but they are separated from God's presence and power, which is eternal death.

"And to you who are troubled rest with us, when the Lord Jesus shall be
revealed from heaven with His mighty angels, In flaming fire taking
vengeance on them that know not God, and that obey not the gospel of
our Lord Jesus Christ: Who shall be punished with everlasting destruction
from the presence of the Lord, and from the glory of His power."
2 Thessalonians 1:7-9

"And they shall go forth, and look upon the carcases of the men that have transgressed against Me: for their worm shall not die, neither shall their fire be quenched; and they shall be an abhorring unto all flesh."
Isaiah 66:24

According to Scripture, this indicates conscious, eternal torment.

In Revelation 19:20, the first residents of Gehenna seem to be the Beast and the False Prophet. John said,

"And I saw the beast, and the kings of the earth, and their armies, gathered together to make war against Him that sat on the horse, and against His army. And the beast was taken, and with him the false prophet that wrought miracles before him, with which he deceived them that had received the mark of the beast, and them that worshipped his image. These both were cast alive *into a lake of fire burning with brimstone."*
Revelation 19:19,20

On this earth, Satan knows he has only a short time to continue to deceive mankind.

"And the great dragon was cast out, that old serpent, called the Devil, and Satan, which deceiveth the whole world: he was cast out into the earth, and his angels were cast out with him."
Revelation 12:9

"... for the devil is come down unto you, having great wrath, because he knoweth that he hath but a short time."
Revelation 12:12

During the ministry of Jesus, the demons were always crying out not to be punished and tormented before the time.

"... there met Him two possessed with devils [demons] ... And, behold, they cried out, saying, What have we to do with thee, Jesus, thou Son of God? art Thou come hither to torment us before the time?"
Matthew 8:28,29

"... there met Him out of the city a certain man, which had devils [demons] long time ... When he saw Jesus, he cried out, and fell down before Him, and with a loud voice said, What have I to do with Thee, Jesus, thou Son of God most high? I beseech Thee, torment me not."
Luke 8:27,28

Hell was created for Satan and the other fallen angels who followed him in rebellion. The unsaved of humanity from all ages who have rejected Christ, will be with them in this place of torment.

"Then shall he say also unto them on the left hand, Depart from me,
ye cursed, into everlasting fire, **prepared for the devil and his angels.**
And these shall go away into everlasting punishment .... "
Matthew 25:41,46

"And shall cast them into a furnace of fire:
there shall be wailing and gnashing of teeth."
Matthew 13:42

Those who rejected Christ and are in the temporary abode of the dead called Hades, will be raised and judged at the Great White Throne Judgment; then, will be cast into the Lake of Fire [Gehenna] as their final destination. This is the everlasting reward of all that die in their sins.

"And I saw the dead, small and great, stand before God;
and the books were opened: and another book was opened,
which is the Book of Life: and the dead were judged out of those
things which were written in the books, according to their works.

And the sea gave up the dead which were in it; and death [thanatos]
and Hell [Hades] delivered up the dead which were in them: and they
were judged every man according to their works. And death and Hell
were cast into the Lake of Fire. This is the Second Death. And whosoever
was not found written in the Book of Life was cast into the Lake of Fire."
Revelation 20:12-15

Test Your Knowledge

*** All answers to the following questions can be found within the pages of this chapter or the Answer Key (at the back of the book).

CHALLENGE YOURSELF: Test your knowledge without referring to the Answer Key

Chapter 14 – Hell = Gehenna

1. There are others that spoke more of *Gehenna* than Jesus.
   a. True
   b. False

2. How many times is the New Testament Greek word *Gehenna* found in the Bible?
   a. 5
   b. 15
   c. 12
   d. 21

3. Gehenna is the place of future punishment of the unrepentant angels and unbelievers (those who have not invited Jesus into their hearts) for all eternity.
   a. True
   b. False

4. The Lake of Fire and the Second Death are not related to one another.
   a. True
   b. False

5. In the Old Testament, horrible idolatrous practices where children were sacrificed took place at this location:
   a. Valley of Dry Bones
   b. Valley of Hinnom
   c. Valley of Shadow of Death
   d. Valley of Wailing Wall

6. The answer to question #5 symbolizes which place of punishment for the wicked?
   a. Hades
   b. Sheol
   c. Gehenna
   d. Qeber

7. Which King in question #5 burned his children in the fire?
   a. King Ahaz
   b. King of Egypt
   c. King of Assyria
   d. King David

8. Jesus deliberately used the word Gehenna to impress upon His hearers that ____________ __________________, as a ________________of sin, awaits the _______________ after the resurrection.

9. Jesus said in Matthew chapter ____ verse ____, "… but rather fear Him which is able to destroy both soul and body in Hell [Gehenna]."

10. The Greek word which means to destroy, to be delivered up to eternal misery, is which of the following?

    a. Thanatos

    b. Mnema

    c. Taphos

    d. Apollumi

11. Where does it say that, "And death [thanatos] and Hell [Hades] were cast into the Lake of Fire [Gehenna]. This is the Second Death."

    a. Revelation 12:12

    b. 2 Thessalonians 1:7

    c. Revelation 20:14

    d. Luke 12:5

12. On this earth, Satan knows that he has only a ___________________, to continue to _______________ mankind.

13. During the ministry of Jesus, the demons (fallen angels) were always crying out not to be _________________ and __________________ before the time.

14. According to Revelation 19:19, 20, the first Resident(s) of Gehenna to be (cast alive) into a lake of fire burning with brimstone seem to be ...

    a. the Kings of the earth and their armies

    b. the Beast

    c. the False Prophet

    d. b and c

15. Where will those who rejected Christ and are in the (temporary abode) of the dead called Hades, be raised and judged?

    a. Judgment Seat of Christ

    b. Pearly Gates

    c. Great White Throne Judgment

    d. a and b

16. According to Matthew chapter _____ verse _____, Hell was created or prepared for Satan and the other fallen angels who followed him in rebellion.

17. Sheol and Hades (both) describe the temporary abode of the dead until the resurrection.

    a. True

    b. False

18. Revelation 20:12 says, "And I saw the dead, small and great, stand before God; the _________ were __________: and another __________ was __________, which is the ______________________________ … ."

19. In the Book of Revelation, How did it say the dead were judged out of those things which were written in the Book of Life?

    a. By their good outweighing their bad

    b. By how many times they went to Confession

    c. According to their regular attendance at Church or Mass

    d. According to their works

20. Where did God say the Final Destination will be for everybody whose name was not found written in the Book of Life?

    a. Gehenna

    b. Tartaroo

    c. The Lake of Fire

    d. Sheol

    e. a and c

GRADE SCALE

Missed 0-2 = Excellent
Missed 3-4 = Very Good
Missed 5-6 = Good
Missed 7 = Average
Mised 8 or more = Need to Re-read Chapter

☐ Excellent
☐ Very Good
☐ Good
☐ Average
☐ Need to Re-read Chapter

15

Hell = Paradise

Paradise - comes from the Greek word *paradeisos [pä-rä'-dā-sos].* Paradise at one time was the part of Hell [Sheol/Hades] whereby the souls/spirits of the righteous awaited.

There wasn't much knowledge of the afterlife in the Old Testament. Therefore, nothing was said about Paradise in the Old Testament. It wasn't mentioned until Jesus came in the New Testament and talked about this blessed place in the underworld below.

Before Christ ascended into Heaven, believers as well as unbelievers were said to enter Sheol or Hades. Until Christ accomplished His work on the Cross, even those who loved God (the righteous dead) could not go to Heaven.

The Greek word for Heaven is *ouranos [ü-rä-no's],* which has two meanings.

1. The vaulted expanse of the sky with all things visible in it (sky, clouds, stars, etc.).
2. The region above the sidereal heavens, the seat of order of things eternal and consummately perfect where God and other heavenly beings dwell.

During His earthly ministry, Jesus said,

"And no man hath ascended up to Heaven, but He that came down from Heaven, even the Son of man which is in Heaven."
John 3:13

Since this statement was made by the Lord Jesus at the time of His 3-year ministry on earth, we can conclude that no Old Testament saint who had died (at that point) ascended into the third Heaven.

However, the Scriptures make mention of two men (Enoch and Elijah) who did not experience physical death. God's Word says that,

"By faith Enoch was translated that he should not see death ... ."
Hebrews 11:5

"And it came to pass, as they still went on, and talked, that, behold, there appeared a chariot of fire, and horses of fire, and parted them both asunder; and Elijah went up by a whirlwind into heaven [shamayim]."
II Kings 2:11

The Hebrew word *shamayim [shä·mah'·yim]* is the Old Testament word for Heaven. It also means:

1. Visible heavens, universe, sky, atmosphere, etc.

2. Heaven (as the abode of God)

Even though Enoch and Elijah did not die, because Jesus said 'no man hath ascended into Heaven' as yet, they had to have gone some place other than the third Heaven, which is the abode of God. Then, where did they go? Let's see.

In Old Testament times, the sacrifices that were offered were temporary that pointed to the ultimate sacrifice of Christ. The blood of animals shed in Hebrew religious ceremonies (only temporarily) covered their sins. Those sacrifices were not able to wash away their sin; only the blood of Christ can do this. As it is written,

"For it is not possible that the blood of bulls and of goats should take away sins."
Hebrews 10:4

Therefore, it appears that the departed souls/spirits (all righteous believers) were held in a temporary compartment in the underworld of Hell below in a place called Paradise.

From New Testament teaching, we see that Sheol/Hades was divided into at least two compartments. One was a place of torment while the other was a place of comfort, which was referred to as Abraham's Bosom.

"And it came to pass, that the beggar died, and was carried by the angels into Abraham's bosom: the rich man also died, and was buried; And in Hell [Hades] he lift up his eyes, being in torments, and seeth Abraham afar off, and Lazarus in his bosom."
Luke 16:22,23

Also, Jesus said to one of the thieves on the Cross,

"... Verily I say unto thee, Today shalt thou be with Me in Paradise."
Luke 23:43

The Paradise of Eden which man lost in the Garden, seems to have become the name for a certain compartment of Sheol/Hades - a place for the souls/spirits of the righteous dead. Though it was beautiful enough to be called Paradise, and referred to as Abraham's Bosom; it was not Heaven.

According to David and also Peter, Jesus Himself went to Sheol/Hades, during the interval between His death and the resurrection of His body.

"For Thou wilt not leave My soul in Hell [Sheol] .... ."
Psalm 16:10

"... His soul was not left in Hell [Hades] .... ."
Acts 2:31

Jesus was quite busy in the spiritual underworld, while His body was in the tomb. His soul/spirit was not in Hell Fire, but He went to the Paradise side where the righteous resided. Peter said,

"By which also He went and preached unto the spirits in prison."
I Peter 3:19

Paul describes Christ's descent into Hell (Paradise side).

"... what is it but that He also descended first into the lower parts of the earth?"
Ephesians 4:9

Paul is not talking about the sepulcher or the grave. No grave is in the lower parts of the earth. If anything, the physical body of Jesus was laid horizontally in a tomb which was excavated out of a great rock in the mountain side.

Paul goes on to say,

"Wherefore He saith, When He ascended up on high,
He led captivity captive ... ."
Ephesians 4:8

Who Where the Captives?

The Old Testament and New Testament saints who died before the death of Christ, were held captive in the Paradise compartment in Sheol/Hades. They were there (waiting for the ultimate sacrifice to be made) which would go beyond just covering their sin, but actually taking away their sin. The Hebrew writer states,

"... but now once in the end of the world hath
He appeared to put away sin by the sacrifice of Himself."
Hebrews 9:26

The believers were captive in the sense of being restricted and confined there (in Paradise) until the Lord Jesus Christ would die for the sins of the whole world. After Jesus fulfilled His mission, the believers were (then eligible) to be released for entrance into Heaven to be with Him.

When Jesus Christ rose from the dead He ascended to the Father, taking the saints who were in Abraham's Bosom (Paradise) to Heaven with Him. As Jesus ascended on high, He lead those captive believers from one destination to another. What joy, as the Son arrives back with the Father and with Him the spoils (captives) of victory. The prophet Isaiah speaks of the Messiah (Jesus) by saying,

"... Behold I and the children whom God hath given Me."
Hebrews 2:13

"The chariots of God are twenty thousand, even thousands of angels:
the Lord is among them, as in Sinai, in the Holy Place. Thou hast ascended
on high, thou hast led captivity captive: thou hast received gifts for men; yea,
for the rebellious also, that the LORD God might dwell among them."
Psalm 68:17,18

Paradise was not in Heaven before the cross, for Jesus testified to the women on the morning He was resurrected that He had not yet gone up to His Father.

"Jesus saith unto her, Touch Me not; for I am not yet ascended to My Father: but go to My brethren, and say unto them, I ascend unto My Father, and your Father; and to My God, and your God."
John 20:17

By the time Paul wrote the Epistle of Second Corinthians, Paradise had already been taken out of Hades and was now placed in the third Heaven. Paul said,

"I knew a man in Christ above fourteen years ago, (whether in the body, I cannot tell; or whether out of the body, I cannot tell: God knoweth;) such an one caught up to the third Heaven. And I knew such a man, (whether in the body, or out of the body, I cannot tell: God knoweth;) How that he was caught up into Paradise [Paradeisos], and heard unspeakable words, which it is not lawful for a man to utter."
2 Corinthians 12:2-4

As of now, Paradise has been moved and is later mentioned in connection with the Tree of Life.

"He that hath an ear, let him hear what the Spirit saith unto the churches; To him that overcometh will I give to eat of the Tree of Life, which is in the midst of the Paradise of God."
Revelation 2:7

"And he shewed me a pure river of water of life, clear as crystal, proceeding out of the throne of God and of the Lamb. In the midst of the street of it, and on either side of the river, was there the Tree of Life, which bare twelve manner of fruits, and yielded her fruit every month: and the leaves of the tree were for the healing of the nations."
Revelation 22:1,2

Clearly, Paradise is the place where souls/spirits of believers go immediately after death. Paul says this with confidence,

"We are confident, I say, and willing rather to be absent from the body, and to be present with the Lord."
2 Corinthians 5:8

Test Your Knowledge

*** All answers to the following questions can be found within the pages of this chapter or the Answer Key (at the back of the book).

CHALLENGE YOURSELF: Test your knowledge without referring to the Answer Key

Chapter 15 – Hell = Paradise

1. The Old Testament is full of information about Paradise.
   a. True
   b. False

2. Two men who did not experience death were:
   a. Elijah and Joshua
   b. Enoch and Moses
   c. Elijah and Enoch
   d. Aaron and Moses

3. From New Testament teaching, we see that Sheol/Hades was divided into at least two compartments. One was a place of ___________ and the other was a place of ___________.

4. Paradise has now been moved from below and is mentioned in connection with what tree:
   a. Tree of the Knowledge of Good and of Evil
   b. Fig tree
   c. Tree of Life
   d. Apple Tree

5. The three days and nights in which Jesus was dead, His body, soul, and spirit never left the tomb.
   a. True
   b. False

6. When Jesus ascended on high, He took the captive saints with Him.
   a. True
   b. False

7. Who was the first person to mention the word Paradise?
   a. Isaiah
   b. David
   c. Matthew
   d. Jesus

8. The Greek word for Heaven in the New Testament of the King James Version is.....
   a. Shamayim
   b. Mnemeion
   c. Ouranos
   d. Kiometerion

9. The Hebrew word for Heaven in the Old Testament of the King James Version is.....
   a. Shamayim
   b. Paradeisos
   c. Ouranos
   d. Kiometerion

10. Which of the following describe the "Heavens"?
    a. The sky and the clouds
    b. The stars or constellations
    c. The region above the stars (the abode of God-where God dwells)
    d. All of the above

11. In Old Testament times, the sacrifices (the blood of animals) that were offered were ____________________ that pointed to the ultimate sacrifice of Christ.

12. The departed souls/spirits of those who loved and served God (before Jesus arose) were held in a "temporary compartment" in the underworld of Hell which was referred to as which of the following?
    a. Abraham's Bosom
    b. The abode of God
    c. Paradise
    d. Ouranos
    e. Shamayim
    f. a and c
    g. a, c, d, and e

13. Which scriptures below confirm that Jesus' soul/spirit was NOT in the torment side of Hell but in the side (compartment) of Hell where the righteous souls/spirits resided?
    a. Matthew 17:1
    b. Luke 23:43
    c. 1 Peter 3:19
    d. Ephesians 4:9
    e. b, c, and d

14. After the Resurrection, when Jesus ascended up on High (to the third Heaven), he took (The Old Testament and New Testament saints who died before the death of Christ) the "Righteous" souls/spirits back with him.

    Which scripture does NOT refer to leading *captivity captive*?

    a. Ephesians 4:8

    b. Hebrews 2:13

    c. Hebrews 10:4

    d. Psalm 68:18

15. By the time Paul wrote the Epistle of ____________________, Paradise had been taken out of Hades and was now placed in the

    ________________________.

HOW WELL DID YOU DO?

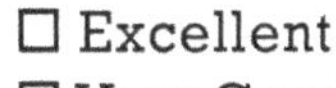

GRADE SCALE

Missed 0-1 = Excellent
Missed 2 = Very Good
Missed 3 = Good
Missed 4-5 = Average
Mised 6 or more = Need to Re-read Chapter

☐ Excellent
☐ Very Good
☐ Good
☐ Average
☐ Need to Re-read Chapter

16

The Rich Man & Lazarus

Death has always been a terror and a mystery. Very little was said about what happens inside Sheol or Hades in Scripture *until* Jesus came and let us know *exactly* what lies behind death's door, in the afterlife of the spirit underworld.

Jesus gave us the story of the rich man and the beggar Lazarus. The majority of the questions that we have about death and the afterlife can be answered in the account of this story.

If you carefully examine what the entire Bible says about death and the afterlife, you will find that everything in this story fits. It is consistent with the overall teaching about death and the afterlife.

There are some who contend that this is only a parable and that this parable never actually took place. There are also attempts to treat this as a completely symbolic parable that teaches anything (but) death or the afterlife.

Those who hold to a position of soul-sleep or the eradication of the soul at death, usually end up with farfetched interpretations. When they try to explain away what this story actually says, they clearly violate other doctrinal passages on the subjects of death and the afterlife.

There is nothing that says this is a parable. Many, including myself, hold the position that this is a realistic event because this story uses the actual names of people. Nevertheless, whether this is a true incident or parable, the teaching behind it remains the same. Jesus uses this story to plainly teach that after death, there is fully functioning consciousness.

The Scriptures teach that it is the body that sleeps and returns to dust, but the internal soul/spirit departs at death and awaits resurrection; either in comfort or torment.

In this story, we have the afterlife conversation that takes place between the rich man who died and Abraham. This conversation did not take place in the grave. We can clearly see that these men were in a place of departed souls/spirits rather than a burial place.

Jesus says this story actually took place and this is how He told it:

> *"There <u>was</u> a certain rich man, which was clothed in purple and fine linen, and fared sumptuously every day: And there was a certain beggar named Lazarus, which was laid at his gate, full of sores, And desiring to be fed with the crumbs which fell from the rich man's table: moreover the dogs came and licked his sores.*
>
> *And it came to pass, that the beggar died, and was carried by the angels into Abraham's bosom: the rich man also died, and was buried [grave]; And in Hell [Sheol] he lift up his eyes, being in torments, and seeth Abraham afar off, and Lazarus in his bosom.*
>
> *And he cried and said, Father Abraham, have mercy on me, and send Lazarus, that he may dip the tip of his finger in water, and cool my tongue; for I am tormented in this flame. But Abraham said, Son, remember that thou in thy lifetime receivedst thy good things, and likewise Lazarus evil things: but now he is comforted, and thou art tormented. And beside all this, between us and you there is a great gulf fixed: so that they which would pass from hence to you cannot; neither can they pass to us, that would come from thence.*
>
> *Then he said, I pray thee therefore, father, that thou wouldest send him to my father's house: For I have five brethren; that he may testify unto them, lest they also come into this place of torment. Abraham saith unto him, They have Moses and the prophets; let them hear them. And he said, Nay, father Abraham: but if one went unto them from the dead, they will repent. And he said unto him, If they hear not Moses and the prophets, neither will they be persuaded, though one rose from the dead."*
>
> *Luke 16:19-31*

In this passage, we do not see that the soul/spirit is asleep, but both men are in a state of consciousness. They are in two different places by which they are separated by a great impassable gulf between them. The two realms of Hell [Hades] are described as one side being a place of torment and the other side (Abraham's Bosom) being a place of comfort.

I. Facts About the Believer (Lazarus) at Death

- His Soul/Spirit is immediately carried (escorted) by angels into Hell (Abraham's Bosom)
- His troubles from his previous earthly life were passed away
- He is in the presence of Abraham (the father of faith)
- He is experiencing an afterlife of comfort and happiness
- He does not seem to notice the other side of Hell/Hades
- He does not seem to be troubled about the terrible hardship of the rich man

II. Facts About the Unbeliever (the Rich Man) at Death

- He immediately finds himself being tormented in some type of flame
- He is able to see and sees the glory of the Paradise side of Hell
- He looks and recognizes Lazarus on the other side with Abraham
- He (from across the great gulf) has a conversation with Abraham
- He has a tongue and a desire for water that cannot be quenched
- He cries for mercy and asks for Lazarus' assistance
- He (still) retains his memory from his past life of wrongs
- He never asks to get out; he knows his condition cannot be remedied
- He does not want others to come where he is
- He asks for repentance to be preached to his earthly living family members
- His requests were (all) denied; his earthly life was where decisions were to be made

From looking at this text, we can clearly see that this place called Abraham's Bosom is the place of "Paradise" that Jesus promised to the repentant thief on the cross who asked to be remembered. Jesus said,

"Verily I say unto thee, Today shalt thou be with Me in Paradise."
Luke 23:43

Before Jesus ascended back to the Father, Paradise was the place where the souls/spirits of the righteous dead went when they died.

It's comforting to know that trouble doesn't last always. After the fatigues and troubles of this present life, believers have greater things in store for them.

Lord, thank You for showing us what's beyond death's door.

Test Your Knowledge

*** All answers to the following questions can be found within the pages of this chapter or the Answer Key (at the back of the book).

CHALLENGE YOURSELF: Test your knowledge without referring to the Answer Key

Chapter 16 – The Rich Man & Lazarus

1. Jesus said that the story of the Rich man and the beggar Lazarus was a parable.

   a. True

   b. False

2. The conversation that took place between the rich man and Abraham was:

   a. in the tomb

   b. just before they died

   c. in Hell

   d. while one of them was dreaming

3. At death, the beggar Lazarus had an angelic escort into ______________ ______________.

4. The rich man *lifted his eyes* in the grave.

   a. True

   b. False

5. The rich man (in Hell) wanted someone to go to his family members and ________________ so they too would not come to that terrible place.

6. There was a great impassable gulf between the two compartments of Hades.

   a. True

   b. False

7. Jesus uses the story of this rich man and the beggar Lazarus to plainly teach that after death, there is fully ____________________________.

8. How many brothers did the rich man (in Hell) fear would be joining him in the place of torment, if he couldn't get a special message to them?

   a. 3

   b. 2

   c. 5

   d. 4

9. In Luke chapter _____ verse ____ it says that a person in the torment side (compartment) of Hell CANNOT pass to the comfort side (compartment) where the righteous souls/spirits resided before Jesus' death.

10. How many facts were listed in the sections titled "Facts about the Believer (Lazarus) at death" and "Facts about the Unbeliever (the Rich Man) at death"?

    a. Lazarus (7), Rich Man (11)

    b. Lazarus (6), Rich Man (10)

    c. Lazarus (5), Rich Man (12)

    d. Lazarus (6), Rich Man (11)

GRADE SCALE

Missed 0 = Excellent
Missed 1 = Very Good
Missed 2 = Good
Missed 3 = Average
Mised 4 or more = Need to Re-read Chapter

HOW WELL DID YOU DO?

☐ Excellent
☐ Very Good
☐ Good
☐ Average
☐ Need to Re-read Chapter

17

The Resurrection

Old Testament believers had an imperfect and incomplete knowledge of what happened to a person at the time of death. Sheol was the all-purpose word used to describe the place where souls/spirits of both believers and unbelievers went.

Saints from the earliest of times believed there would be a general resurrection at the end of the world; then, there would be a final judgment.

Lets take a look at scriptures (by Abraham, Job, King David, Daniel, the Hebrew writer, and Jesus Himself) concerning the resurrection.

Abraham believed that God was able to raise the dead, and was willing to sacrifice his son in obedience to God.

"Accounting that God was able
to raise him [Isaac] up, even from the dead ... ."
Hebrews 11:19

Job believed in the resurrection, he said,

"For I know that my Redeemer liveth, and that He shall stand
at the latter day upon the earth: And though after my skin worms
destroy this body, yet in my flesh shall I see God: Whom
I shall see for myself, and mine eyes shall behold, and not another ... ."
Job 19:25-27

King David believed in the resurrection, he said,

"But God will redeem my soul from the power of the Grave [Sheol]: for He shall receive me. Selah"
Psalm 49:15

Daniel believed in the resurrection for both believers and unbelievers, he said,

"And many of them that sleep in the dust of the earth shall awake, some to everlasting life, and some to shame and everlasting contempt."
Daniel 12:2

The Hebrew writer spoke of many that endured incredible hardships because they believed in the resurrection, saying,

"Women received their dead raised to life again: and others were tortured, not accepting deliverance; that they might obtain a better resurrection."
Hebrews 11:35

In Scripture, sleep is used to describe the bodies of departed Christians. Our English word *cemetery* comes from the Greek word koimeterion *[koimētḗrion]* which means *sleeping place.*

Sleep is an appropriate simile of death, because the deceased person appears to be sleeping. In this physical life, when we go to sleep, we act out this symbol of death; when we awake, it is like a resurrection.

In the New Testament, the Pharisees and Sadducees were bitterly divided upon the question of bodily resurrection. The Sadducees did not believe in a future resurrection. They were constantly in conflict with Jesus and the Apostles.

"Then come unto Him the Sadducees, which say there is no resurrection ... ."
Mark 12:18

"... and the Sadducees, came upon them, Being grieved that they taught the people, and preached through Jesus the resurrection from the dead."
Acts 4:1,2

At different times, Apostle Paul made it a point to distinguish his faith in the resurrection of the dead from the view of the Sadducees. In the Acts of the Apostles, it says,

"But when Paul perceived that the one part were Sadducees, and the other Pharisees, he cried out in the council, Men and brethren, I am a Pharisee, the son of a Pharisee: of the hope and resurrection of the dead I am called in question. And when he had so said, there arose a dissension between the Pharisees and the Sadducees: and the multitude was divided. For the Sadducees say that there is no resurrection, neither angel, nor spirit: but the Pharisees confess both."
Acts 23:6-8

"Why should it be thought a thing incredible with you, that God should raise the dead?"
Acts 26:8

New Testament Resurrections (by Jesus)

The most powerful testimony and authority concerning the resurrection of the dead was spoken by Jesus Christ. He (not only spoke of the resurrection), but He demonstrated it by raising a few people from the dead by the sheer command of His word. Listed below are a few examples:

I. Jairus' Daughter

"While He yet spake, there cometh one from the ruler of the synagogue's house, saying to him, Thy daughter is dead; trouble not the Master. And all wept, and bewailed her: but He said, Weep not; she is not dead, but sleepeth. And they laughed Him to scorn, knowing that she was dead. And He put them all out, and took her by the hand, and called, saying, Maid, arise. And her spirit came again, and she arose straightway: and He commanded to give her meat."
Luke 8:49,52-55

II. Widow's Son

"Now when He came nigh to the gate of the city, behold, there was a dead man carried out, the only son of his mother, and she was a widow: and much people of the city was with her. And when the Lord saw her, He had compassion on her, and said unto her, Weep not. And He came and touched the bier: and they that bare him stood still. And He said, Young man, I say unto thee, Arise. And he that was dead sat up, and began to speak. And He delivered him to his mother."
Luke 7:12-15

III. Lazarus

"And some of them said, Could not this man, which opened the eyes of the blind, have caused that even this man should not have died? Jesus said, Take ye away the stone. Martha, the sister of him that was dead, saith unto him, Lord, by this time he stinketh: for he hath been dead four days. And when He thus had spoken, He cried with a loud voice, Lazarus, come forth. And he that was dead came forth, bound hand and foot with graveclothes: and his face was bound about with a napkin. Jesus saith unto them, Loose him, and let him go."
John 11:37,39,43,44

Yet, the greatest and most important example came from Jesus when He proved the dead shall live again by His own resurrection. Death, Hell, and the Grave could not hold Him. He conquered them all, and arose with all power in His hands.

After Jesus arose from the dead, He confirmed that He was alive by physically appearing to the Apostles (as well as) talking to them about the Kingdom of God. In Acts it says,

"To whom also He shewed Himself alive after His passion by many infallible proofs, being seen of them forty days, and speaking of the things pertaining to the Kingdom of God."
Acts 1:3

Christ rose bodily from the grave with a real body with supernatural powers that could be seen and handled. He proved His identity by the nail prints in His hands and feet and the spear print in His side. Interestingly, although His body required no food; Jesus could eat.

"Then the same day at evening, being the first day of the week, when the doors were shut where the disciples were assembled for fear of the Jews, came Jesus and stood in the midst, and saith unto them, Peace be unto you."
John 20:19

"And after eight days again His disciples were within, and Thomas with them: then came Jesus, the doors being shut, and stood in the midst, and said, Peace be unto you. Then saith He to Thomas, Reach hither thy finger, and behold My hands; and reach hither thy hand, and thrust it into My side: and be not faithless, but believing. And Thomas answered and said unto Him, My Lord and my God."
John 20:26-28

"Behold My hands and My feet, that it is I myself: handle Me,
and see; for a spirit hath not flesh and bones, as ye see Me have."
Luke 24:39

"Him God raised up the third day, and shewed Him openly;
Not to all the people, but unto witnesses chosen before of God,
even to us, who did eat and drink with Him after He rose from the dead."
Acts 10:40,41

"And they gave Him a piece of a broiled fish, and of an honeycomb.
And He took it, and did eat before them."
Luke 24:42,43

"... and they knew Him; and He vanished out of their sight."
Luke 24:31

Jesus arose with a glorified, incorruptible, mighty, spiritual, heavenly body. He arose and so shall we.

On the Mount of Transfiguration, the curtain was drawn aside (momentarily) to give us an idea of what our glorified body will be like. As Jesus was seen in a dazzling display of brightness; one day, so shall we. The following scriptures shows the resemblance,

"And was transfigured before them: and His face did shine as the sun,
and His raiment was white as the light."
Matthew 17:2

"And as we have borne the image of the earthy,
we shall also bear the image of the heavenly."
I Corinthians 15:49

"Then shall the righteous
shine forth as the sun in the Kingdom of their Father."
Matthew 13:43

"And they that be wise shall shine as the brightness of the firmament;
and they that turn many to righteousness as the stars for ever and ever."
Daniel 12:3

At the return of Christ, we believers shall be like Him.

"Who shall change our vile body,
that it may be fashioned like unto His glorious body ... ."
Philippians 3:21

The Firstfruit

Jesus Christ rose from the dead and He is called "the Firstfruits of them that slept."

"But now is Christ risen from the dead, and become the Firstfruits of them that slept. But every man in his own order: Christ the Firstfruits; afterward they that are Christ's at His coming."
1 Corinthians 15:20,23

Firstfruits implies and involves a similar situation all *will experience* who are to follow the pattern of Jesus Christ. All those who have died in Christ Jesus will share in His triumph over the grave.

When Adam sinned, he lost spiritual fellowship with God which resulted in spiritual death. Immediately, his body began to age and eventually it returned to dust (physical death).

In this life, we all are tormented with some type of suffering. We are constantly putting up with breakdowns of this mortal, corrupt flesh. This poor old rickety body is always in need of some type of doctoring; then, it dies.

At death, the natural body is sown in corruption or goes to the grave in the weakness of pain and often times agonies. Sin robbed the body of God's original intention. But sin and death will not triumph over the body of the believer to the extent of corruption, retaining possession of our flesh forever. This body will be restored and one day will live again, but only after it has undergone a change. It will be renovated at the coming of the Lord Jesus Christ. He will give this body a robe of glory (more beautiful) beyond anything we can conceive. One day, we will be wholly conformed to the body of His glory.

At the sound of the trumpet of God, the graves of the bodies of believers in Christ that are asleep (that have returned to dust), shall be raised from the dead.

"For as in Adam all die, even so in Christ shall all be made alive."
I Corinthians 15:22

This natural body will be replaced by a spiritual body. This shaky frame will be repaid for all it has suffered. Paul says,

"For I reckon that the sufferings of this present time are not worthy to be compared with the glory which shall be revealed in us."
Romans 8:18

"So also is the resurrection of the dead. It is sown in corruption; it is raised in incorruption: It is sown in dishonour; it is raised in glory: it is sown in weakness; it is raised in power: It is sown a natural body; it is raised a spiritual body. There is a natural body, and there is a spiritual body."
I Corinthians 15:42-44

The Scripture points to the time when, one moment we are here (on earth) in these weak and worn bodies; then the next moment, we'll be there (in Heaven) in bodies powerful and glorious. What a day of rejoicing that will be! Paul goes on to say,

"And as we have borne the image of the earthy, we shall also bear the image of the heavenly."
I Corinthians 15:49

To paraphrase Paul, there is one body for the soul here (on earth), and another body for spirit up there (in Heaven). The body is the same in identity, but not in the same glory (magnificence, majestic beauty, brightness, splendor). As a necessity, the body will be changed to meet the new conditions.

"It is sown in dishonour; it is raised in glory: it is sown in weakness; it is raised in power: It is sown a natural body; it is raised a spiritual body. There is a natural body, and there is a spiritual body. For this corruptible must put on incorruption, and this mortal [must] put on immortality."
I Corinthians 15:43,44,53

Hallelujah - those who are alive when Jesus comes will have victory over death by being changed from mortality to immortality, in the twinkling of an eye.

"In a moment, in the twinkling of an eye, at the last trump: for the trumpet shall sound, and the dead shall be raised incorruptible, and we shall be changed."
I Corinthians 15:52

Return of Christ For The Living and The Dead

The believers in Christ who have died and whose souls/spirits are with Jesus, shall be with Him when He comes to get the rest of His body of believers.

"For if we believe that Jesus died and rose again,
even so them also which sleep in Jesus will God bring with Him."
I Thessalonians 4:14

"In a moment, in the twinkling of an eye, at the last trump: for the trumpet shall sound, and the dead shall be raised incorruptible, and we shall be changed. For this corruptible must put on incorruption, and this mortal [must] put on immortality. So when this corruptible shall have put on incorruption, and this mortal shall have put on immortality, then shall be brought to pass the saying that is written, Death is swallowed up in victory. O death, where [is] thy sting? O grave, where is thy victory?"
I Corinthians 15:52-55

When Jesus comes, the souls will reunite with the elements of the body and the whole man will be formed once again. The scattered, dry bones shall live. Every atom, every speck, and particle (however far away) will come together again. They shall come forth to live again in the power of an endless life.

The disembodied state (separation of soul/spirit from the body) will not last forever. Our spirit will again be clothed with flesh and bones. Mortality will be swallowed by eternal life. We shall rise in power, restored; standing complete as a whole being, body, soul, and spirit.

As with Christ – we have the same hope. What we will be has not (yet) been made known. We can't conceive what it means to be fully like the glorified Lord Jesus Christ. Our finite minds can't contain it. God's Word says,

"Beloved, now are we the sons of God, and it doth not yet appear
what we shall be: but we know that, when He shall appear,
we shall be like Him; for we shall see Him as He is."
I John 3:2

"For our conversation is in Heaven; from whence also we look for
the Savior, the Lord Jesus Christ: Who shall change our vile body,

that it may be fashioned like unto His glorious body ... ."
Philippians 3:20,21

In our transformed, glorified body, we will bear the likeness of our Redeemer. This should cause us to be expectantly waiting for the Second Coming of our Lord. Those bodies that are asleep in the dust of the earth will experience a bodily resurrection and connect with their souls/spirits that He will bring with Him. Christians alive on earth when Christ returns will find their bodies changed in a flash, in the twinkling of an eye.

Where Christ is - we will be. What Christ is - we will become. What Christ does - we will share.

Death of Death

'The last enemy that shall be destroyed is death."
I Corinthians 15:26

Death cannot be destroyed until the very bones (or remains) of the saints are delivered from the strongholds of the enemy.

"... there shall be a resurrection of the dead, both of the just and unjust."
Acts 24:15

"And the sea gave up the dead which were in it; and Death and Hell delivered up the dead which were in them: and they were judged every man according to their works. And Death and Hell were cast into the Lake of Fire ... ."
Revelation 20:13,14

Resurrection Of The Unsaved

Whenever Jesus spoke of Hell and the lost state of the wicked, He described bodies in misery. Over and over, Jesus clearly warned of going to that awful place called Hell (Gehenna - Lake of Fire).

Hell is a place for bodies as well as for souls/spirits. The wicked will have bodies in Hell and will be the final abode of all those who live and die in their sin.

The certainties are set down so that no man can miss them. God has not hidden it, nor is He silent concerning it. God has written it largely upon the sacred page so that even the simple-minded may read it and understand.

In unmistakable language, the Bible speaks of unending torment for the lost, urging the unsaved to flee from the wrath to come.

The Lake of Fire is a place of conscious suffering. What doom and dreary abode awaits those who die out of Christ. Demons (unclean spirits) are even terrified about going there, as seen in the following scriptures.

"(For He had commanded the unclean spirit to come out of the man. ...). And they besought Him that He would not command them to go out into the deep."
Luke 8:29,31

"And, behold, they cried out, saying, What have we to do with Thee, Jesus, thou Son of God? art Thou come hither to torment us before the time?"
Matthew 8:29

"And shall cast them into the furnace of fire: there shall be wailing and gnashing of teeth."
Matthew 13:50

"Where their worm dieth not [physical suffering], and the fire is not quenched."
Mark 9:44

Acceptance of the finished work of Christ for sinners (alone) guarantees deliverance from the terrible doom depicted by Christ for those who die lost.

Knowing the terror of the Lord, we dare not remain unconcerned or uncaring about the terrible doom of the lost. God says,

"Yet if thou warn the wicked, and he turn not from his wickedness, nor from his wicked way, he shall die in his iniquity; but thou hast delivered thy soul."
Ezekiel 3:19

"Let him know, that he which converteth the sinner from the error of his way shall save a soul from death, and shall hide a multitude of sins."
James 5:20

There will come a time when there will be a bodily resurrection for unbelievers. Their bodies will be raised from the grave or where ever the bodily or dead remains are, and will be reunited with the soul/spirit, which will come out of Sheol/Hades, to be judged. Jesus said,

"Marvel not at this: for the hour is coming, in the which all that are in the graves shall hear His voice, And shall come forth;

... and they that have done evil, unto the resurrection of damnation."
John 5:28,29

"And the sea gave up the dead which were in it;
and Death and Hell [Sheol/Hades] delivered up the dead
which were in them: and they were judged
every man according to their works."
Revelation 20:13

Since the body had a lot to do with sin and sinning; it is only natural that the body should be punished. Body and soul (sinning together) must suffer together in unending misery. Prevention from going to Hell is so serious that Jesus says,

"... if thy right hand offend thee, cut it off, and cast it from thee:
for it is profitable for thee that one of thy members should perish,
and not that thy whole body should be cast into Hell."
Matthew 5:30

There is no picture in Scripture of the type of bodies for those who die without accepting Christ. Though the details are omitted, whatever type of body it is, it will be fitted to endure the quenchless fire of judgment. The body will be prepared in a way to burn forever, yet not be consumed. God has shown in Scripture that this can be done, as seen in the following scriptures,

"And the angel of the LORD appeared unto him in a flame of fire out
of the midst of a bush: and he looked, and, behold, the bush burned
with fire, and the bush was not consumed."
Exodus 3:2

"And in those days shall men seek death, and shall not find it;
and shall desire to die, and death shall flee from them."
Revelation 9:6

If you haven't already, take heed to these solid, stern warnings. Flee from the wrath to come. One day each of us will take our last step. King David said,

"... there is but a step between me and death."
I Samuel 20:3

The only escape from everlasting torment is NOW. The Scripture pleads with us not to put off our decision of accepting Christ as Savior.

"... Today if ye will hear His voice, harden not your hearts."
Hebrews 4:7

"... behold, now is the accepted time; behold, now is the day of salvation."
2 Corinthians 6:2

Come to Jesus, now. Tomorrow may be too late. Give Him your heart Today.

Test Your Knowledge

*** All answers to the following questions can be found within the pages of this chapter or the Answer Key (at the back of the book).

CHALLENGE YOURSELF: Test your knowledge without referring to the Answer Key

Chapter 17 – The Resurrection

1. Cemetery comes from the Greek word *koimeterion* which means ________________________________.

2. Which New Testament group did not believe in the Resurrection:
   a. Pharisees
   b. Herodians
   c. Romans
   d. Sadducees

3. Jesus was seen alive after His resurrection for:
   a. 50 days
   b. 3 months
   c. 40 days
   d. 3 days and 3 nights

4. Doubting Thomas said, "______ _______ and ______ ________," after physically seeing the resurrected Christ.

5. At the return of Christ, our (believers) mortal bodies will be fashioned like unto His glorious body.

   a. True

   b. False

6. The last enemy that shall be destroyed is ___________.

7. The only escape from everlasting torment is:

   a. at the Great White Throne Judgment

   b. Purgatory

   c. Now

   d. Gehenna

8. The Bible gives very descriptive detail of the type of resurrected bodies unbelievers will have.

   a. True

   b. False

9. The most powerful testimony and authority concerning the resurrection of the dead was spoken by ________________________________.

10. Which of the following statements concerning the Resurrection was not made by Job?

    a. "And many of them that sleep in the dust of the earth shall awake, some to everlasting life, and some to shame and everlasting contempt."

    b. "For I know that my Redeemer liveth … ."

    c. "And though after my skin worms destroy this body, yet in my flesh shall I see God:"

    d. a and b

11. Name three individuals from this chapter that Jesus demonstrated the resurrection of the dead, by sheer command of His word.

    a. ____________________________

    b. ____________________________

    c. ____________________________

12. Jesus conquered these (_______________, __________________, and ____________________) when He arose with all power in His hands.

13. After Jesus arose from the dead, what scripture listed below confirms that Jesus was not just a spirit, but He had flesh and bones?

    a. Romans 8:18

    b. Matthew 8:29

    c. Luke 8:17

    d. Luke 24:39

14. Jesus Christ rose from the dead and He is called "________________ of them that slept."

15. All those who have died in Christ Jesus will share in His triumph over the grave. This explanation applies to which of the following scriptures?

    a. 2 Timothy 2:14

    b. Job 34:15

    c. I Corinthians 15:12,14

    d. I Corinthians 15:20,23

16. When Adam sinned, he lost _________________ _______________ with God which resulted in ____________________death. Immediately, his body began to age and eventually it returned to dust (_____________ _____________).

17. What scriptures say that the body of the Believer will be restored and one day will live again, but only after it has undergone a change?

    a. 1 Corinthians 15:56, 58

    b. 1 Corinthians 15:31

    c. 1 Corinthians 15:42-44

    d. None of the above

18. Those who are alive when Jesus returns to Earth will have victory over _____________ by being changed from ____________________ to _________________________ in the ____________________ of an eye.

19. According to 1 Thess. 4:14 and 1 Cor. 15:52-55 .....Those bodies that are asleep in the dust will .....

    - Experience a bodily resurrection and
    - Connect with their souls/spirits that Jesus will bring with Him

    a. True

    b. False

20. "… there shall be a resurrection of the dead, both of the ____________and _____________."

21. The Lake of Fire (Gehenna) is a place of conscious _________________.

22. Which of the statements below is not a part of James 5:20 that says, "Let him know, that he which converteth the sinner from the error of his way shall …

    a. Save a soul from death

    b. Shall hide a multitude of sins

    c. Cause him to receive many crowns and rewards

    d. a and b

23. All dead bodies in the sea shall be resurrected prior to judgment.

    a. True

    b. False

24. Prevention from Hell is so serious that Jesus said, "… if thy right hand __________ thee, ______________________, and cast it from thee: for it is ______________________ for thee that one of thy members should perish, and not that thy whole body be cast _________ __________.

25. One day, each of us will take our last step. Who said, " … there is but a step between me and death?"

    a. King Solomon

    b. Apostle Paul

    c. King David

    d. John

HOW WELL DID YOU DO?

GRADE SCALE

Missed 0-2 = Excellent
Missed 3-4 = Very Good
Missed 5-6 = Good
Missed 7 = Average
Mised 8 or more = Need to Re-read Chapter

☐ Excellent
☐ Very Good
☐ Good
☐ Average
☐ Need to Re-read Chapter

18

Heavenly Courtroom

Unless the Lord tarries, one day we (all) will die. But death is not the end. God says,

"And as it is appointed unto men once to die, but after this the judgment."
Hebrews 9:27

"But the LORD shall endure for ever: He hath prepared His throne for judgment. And He shall judge the world in righteousness, He shall minister judgment to the people in uprightness."
Psalm 9:7,8

One day, there will be no choice, all will be hauled forcibly into the Heavenly Courtroom. There will be no contempt for not showing up, because everybody will show up. However, everybody will not be in the same courtroom. There will be two different judgments, one for believers and one for unbelievers.

"For it is written, As I live, saith the Lord, every knee shall bow to Me, and every tongue shall confess to God. So then every one of us shall give account of himself to God."
Romans 14:11,12

"That at the name of Jesus every knee should bow, of things in Heaven, and things in earth, and things under the earth; And that every tongue should confess that Jesus Christ is Lord, to the glory of God the Father."
Philippians 2:10,11

"But I say unto you, That every idle word that men shall speak, they shall give account thereof in the day of judgment. For by thy words thou shalt be justified, and by thy words thou shalt be condemned."
Matthew 12:36,37

While on earth, when Jesus stood before the earthly judge, Pilate did not judge Jesus righteously when He stood before him. With full knowledge of what he was doing, Pilate condemned an innocent man.

"Then Pilate said unto them, Why, what evil hath He done? And they cried out the more exceedingly, Crucify Him. And so Pilate, willing to content the people, released Barabbas unto them, and delivered Jesus, when he had scourged Him, to be crucified."
Mark 15:14,15

The Judge of all the earth – Jesus Christ was illegally tried and judged in order to give mankind the opportunity to have a fair judgment and an Advocate (Intercessor, Defender) present when their day in the Heavenly Court came. John through the Spirit testifies by saying,

"... And if any man sin, we have an Advocate with the Father, Jesus Christ the Righteous."
I John 2:1

The Judge of all the Earth will judge righteously.

"But we are sure that the judgment of God is according to truth against them which commit such things. And thinkest thou this, O man, ... that thou shalt escape the judgment of God? Who will render to every man according to his deeds: Tribulation and anguish, upon every soul of man that doeth evil, of the Jew first, and also of the Gentile; But glory, honour, and peace, to every man that worketh good, to the Jew first, and also to the Gentile: For there is no respect of persons with God."
Romans 2:2,3,6,9-11

No one will ever be able to accuse God of being unfair or unjust. When all is said and done, everybody will know they have been judged righteously.

To prevent mankind from facing the dreaded judgment in the afterlife, the Holy Spirit presses upon the hearts of mankind beforehand that they must meet the God against whom they have sinned and give an account of the deeds done in the body. Then (at that judgment) they will receive the due rewards of those deeds.

The Unsaved In Heavenly Court

In this courtroom, the unsaved will have (already) been condemned. Their sins will testify against them. They will see all the opportunities that God gave them to prepare for eternity. To prevent mankind from making the mistake of being unprepared, through the written Word, God said,

"... but he that believeth not is condemned already, because he hath not believed in the name of the only begotten Son of God. And this is the condemnation, that light is come into the world, and men loved darkness rather than light, because their deeds were evil."
John 3:18,19

"... Son, remember ... ."
Luke 16:25

"And I saw the dead, small and great, stand before God; and the books were opened: and another book was opened, which is the Book]of Life: and the dead were judged out of those things which were written in the books, according to their works."
Revelation 20:12

Everyone will watch as written records are produced and as the evidence concerning their cases is presented to the Judge.

"For nothing is secret, that shall not be made manifest; neither [any thing] hid, that shall not be known and come abroad."
Luke 8:17

The unrighteous will only have a prosecutor, because in the courtroom of The Great White Throne Judgment, all defendants will have previously (in their lifetime) waived their right to an advocate. Their records will be diligently searched. The one witness (JESUS) who can produce the evidence needed to free the defendants, will reject them. Jesus said,

"Many will say to Me in that day, Lord, Lord, have we not prophesied in Thy name? and in Thy name have cast out devils? and in Thy name done many wonderful works? And then will I profess unto them, I never knew you: depart from Me, ye that work iniquity."
Matthew 7:22,23

"But the fearful, and unbelieving, and the abominable, and murderers, and whoremongers, and sorcerers, and idolaters, and all liars, shall have their part in the lake which burneth with fire and brimstone:

which is the Second Death."
Revelation 21:8

Many may not believe now, but one second after unbelievers die (painstakingly) they will realize that Jesus Christ was right about the place called Hell. Once there, there are no Exit signs; you are there — FOREVER!

In this life, everybody (saved and unsaved) will experience the goodness of God in some capacity. Jesus said,

"... your Father which is in Heaven: for He maketh His sun to rise on the evil and on the good, and sendeth rain on the just and on the unjust."
Matthew 5:45

How tragic to be eternally banished from God's blessings, His smile, His glory, and His presence.

"Who shall be punished with everlasting destruction from the presence of the Lord, and from the glory of His power ... ."
2 Thessalonians 1:9

"And these shall go away into everlasting [aionios]punishment ... ."
Matthew 25:46

Aionios [ahee-o'-nee-os] = eternal or of unending duration, without end, never to cease, everlasting.

It is often said that 'things get better with time', however, this is not the case with Hell. Time can never end Hell's torment. Tears can never quench its torment. This is why Paul said,

Knowing therefore the terror of the Lord, we persuade men ... ."
2 Corinthians 5:11

The Righteous In Heavenly Court

For the believer, there will be a different judgment.

"For we must all appear before the Judgment Seat of Christ; that every one may receive the things done in his body, according to that he hath done, whether it be good or bad."
2 Corinthians 5:10

The righteous will have an Advocate (Defense Attorney) provided for them. In the Heavenly Courtroom, the mere presence of the Advocate

(Jesus) guarantees acquittal. The believers will not be concerned about making it; they are already acquitted.

The New Living Translations says,

"... all glory to Him who loves us and has freed us (believers)
from our sins by shedding His blood for us."
Revelation 1:5 NLT

On that great day in the Heavenly Courtroom, what joy it's going to be to have the Righteous, Faithful Witness (JESUS) to represent us (believers) before the Father and all the angels. God said,

"And from Jesus Christ, who is the Faithful Witness ... ."
Revelation 1:5

"... And if any man sin,
we have an Advocate with the Father, Jesus Christ the Righteous."
I John 2:1

"He that overcometh ... I will not blot out his name out of the Book of Life,
but I will confess his name before my Father, and before His angels."
Revelation 3:5

"He that believeth on Him is not condemned ... ."
John 3:18

"There is therefore now no condemnation
to them which are in Christ Jesus ... ."
Romans 8:1

"And this is the record, that God hath given to us eternal life,
and this life is in His Son. He that hath the Son hath life;
and he that hath not the Son of God hath not life."
I John 5:11,12

The scriptures listed in this book (alone) clearly show the holiness of God requires that sin must be punished. For the works done in these earthly bodies, it will either be,

"... Well done, good and faithful servant ... ."
Matthew 25:23
or

"... depart from Me, all ye workers of iniquity."
Luke 13:27

Test Your Knowledge

*** All answers to the following questions can be found within the pages of this chapter or the Answer Key (at the back of the book).

CHALLENGE YOURSELF: Test your knowledge without referring to the Answer Key

Chapter 18 – Heavenly Courtroom

1. After death, there will be the ______________.

2. Everybody will be in one big Heavenly Courtroom together.
   a. True
   b. False

3. One day, every tongue shall confess that Jesus Christ is __________.

4. We must all stand (one day) in God's presence and give an __________ of the _________ done in the body.

5. In the heavenly courtroom, the unsaved:
   a. will have already been condemned
   b. sins will testify against them
   c. will have a chance to repent
   d. a and b

6. The holiness of God requires that sin must be punished.

   a. True

   b. False

7. Where is it written, "And it is appointed unto men once to die, but after this the judgment"?

   a. 1 John 2:1

   b. Mark 15:14

   c. Hebrews 9:27

   d. Revelation 9:6

8. Jesus, the Judge of all the Earth was illegally tried and judged, in order to give mankind the opportunity to have a ____________________ ____________________ and an __________________ (__________________, ________________) present when their day in the Heavenly Court came.

9. The Judge of all the Earth will judge ______________________________.

10. "The sting of death is sin", therefore, to prevent mankind from dreading judgment in the Afterlife - the Holy Spirit presses upon the sinner's heart that he/she must …

    a. Meet the God against whom they have sinned

    b. Be accepting of *all* religions and beliefs to prevent offending others

    c. Give an account of the deeds done in the body

    d. a and c

11. So we wouldn't make the mistake of being unprepared (at the judgment in the Afterlife), the Righteous Judge (God) said in John 3:18, "... but he that ________________ is ____________________ already, because he hath not ______________________ in the name of the only begotten Son of God... ."

12. The unrighteous (those who have not accepted Jesus into their hearts) will only have a _______________, because in the courtroom of the ____, all defendants will have previously (in this life) _______________ their right to an Advocate (Jesus).

13. Matthew 25:46 says, "And these shall go away into everlasting punishment... ." Everlasting means – eternal or of unending duration, without end, and never to cease. Which Greek word below means everlasting in this scripture?

    a. Moros

    b. Phronimos

    c. Nystazo

    d. Aionios

14. In the Heavenly Court, the judgment for the righteous (born-again believers), the righteous will have an Advocate (____________________) provided for them. The mere presence of the Advocate (Jesus) guarantees ____________________.

15. Which of the following scripture verses are NOT included in 1 John 5:11, 12?
    a. "And if any man sin, we have an advocate with the Father, Jesus Christ the Righteous."
    b. "And this is the record, that God hath given to us eternal life, and this life is in His Son."
    c. "For nothing is secret, that shall not be made manifest; neither anything hid, that shall not be known… ."
    d. "He that hath the Son hath life; and he that hath not the Son of God hath not life."
    e. "There is therefore now no condemnation to them which are in Christ Jesus … ."

HOW WELL DID YOU DO?

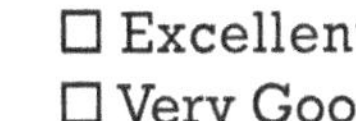

GRADE SCALE

Missed 0-1 = Excellent
Missed 2 = Very Good
Missed 3 = Good
Missed 4-5 = Average
Mised 6 or more = Need to Re-read Chapter

☐ Excellent
☐ Very Good
☐ Good
☐ Average
☐ Need to Re-read Chapter

19

Degrees of Punishment

The Scriptures let us know that everybody will not receive the same judgement. Judgment will be according to works or according to the deeds done while being alive (in the body).

In the Scriptures below, it mentions different degrees of punishment in the afterlife that will be given to unbelievers, some greater - some lesser. Jesus says,

"The lord of that servant will come in a day when he looketh not for him, and at an hour when he is not aware, and will cut him in sunder, and will appoint him his portion with the unbelievers.

And that servant, which knew his lord's will, and prepared not himself, neither did according to his will, shall be beaten with many stripes. *But he that knew not, and did commit things worthy of stripes, shall be beaten with* few stripes.

For unto whomsoever much is given, of him shall be much required: and to whom men have committed much, of him they will ask the more."
Luke 12:46-48

"... the same shall receive greater *damnation."*
Luke 20:47

"Verily I say unto you, It shall be more tolerable for the land of Sodom and Gomorrha in the day of judgment, than for that city."
Matthew 10:15

"And whosoever shall not receive you, nor hear you,
when ye depart thence, shake off the dust under your feet
for a testimony against them. Verily I say unto you,
It shall be more tolerable for Sodom and Gomorrha
in the day of judgment, than for that city."
Mark 6:11

The following phrases were extracted from the scriptures above. Each phrase elevates the punishment to another level or degree.

- More Tolerable
- Few Stripes
- Many Stripes
- Greater Damnation

This is an indication that everybody will not be punished the same.

Other than these Scriptures, not much else is said about how unbelievers will be punished. God has intentionally given all the specifics needed as a warning to avoid the wrath to come.

Even though our finite minds have difficulty understanding God's degrees of punishment; ultimately, God's Word assures us that God is just and fair in all He does. God will do what is right when He judges mankind on that great day.

"And the times of this ignorance God winked at;
but now commandeth all men every where to repent:
Because He hath appointed a day, in the which He will judge
the world in righteousness by that Man whom He hath ordained ... ."
Acts 17:30,31

"That be far from thee to do after this manner, to slay the righteous
with the wicked: and that the righteous should be as the wicked,
that be far from thee: Shall not the Judge of all the earth do right?"
Genesis 18:25

God is good to all. No one will ever be able to accuse God of not giving them a chance. Accept Him and serve Him - while there is still time.

"Knowing therefore the terror of the Lord, we persuade men ... ."
2 Corinthians 5:11

"And with many other words did he testify and exhort, saying, Save yourselves from this untoward [wicked] generation."
Acts 2:40

Test Your Knowledge

*** All answers to the following questions can be found within the pages of this chapter or the Answer Key (at the back of the book).

CHALLENGE YOURSELF: Test your knowledge without referring to the Answer Key

Chapter 19 – Degrees of Punishment

1. In the afterlife, all will receive the same judgment.

   a. True

   b. False

2. The servant in Luke 12 that ___________ not himself, shall be beaten with ___________ stripes.

3. On the appointed day, God will judge the world in ______________.

4. We are called to witness in an attempt to persuade men (mankind), because of the ______________ of the Lord.

5. For unbelievers, there are at least four phrases listed in the scriptures that reveal degrees of punishment. List the four phrases below.

   a. ____________________________

   b. ____________________________

   c. ____________________________

   d. ____________________________

6. God is just in all He does. Which scripture passage below is not a part of Genesis 18:25?

   a. "And the times of this ignorance God winked at; but now commandeth all men everywhere to repent: ..."

   b. "Shall not the Judge of all the earth do right?"

   c. "... And thinkest thou this, O man ... that thou shalt escape the judgment of God?"

   d. a and c

7. The degrees of punishment (in the Afterlife) refers only to the unbeliever.

   a. True

   b. False

8. God has ____________________ given all the ______________________ we need to know as a warning to __________________ the wrath to come.

9. Which Scripture below makes reference to receiver greater damnation (severely punished)?

   a. 1 John 3:2

   b. Ephesians 5:25-27

   c. Revelation 19:7

   d. Luke 20:47

   e. All of the above

10. Judgment will be according to ________________ or according to ________________________ done while being alive (in the body).

HOW WELL DID YOU DO?

GRADE SCALE

Missed 0 = Excellent
Missed 1 = Very Good
Missed 2 = Good
Missed 3 = Average
Mised 4 or more = Need to Re-read Chapter

☐ Excellent
☐ Very Good
☐ Good
☐ Average
☐ Need to Re-read Chapter

20

Future Rewards

Eternal life is not a reward for good works. If our acceptance into Heaven can be earned by anything that we can do, there would've been no need for Jesus to come to Earth and die for us. Jesus Christ paid for our sins on Calvary's Cross. Eternal life is a "free gift" for believing on the risen Savior - the Lord Jesus Christ.

I believe we *all* are interested in payday. Whether we are making $100,000 a year, waiting patiently for a pension, a Social Security check, or $25 weekly from a part-time job - we *all* look forward to receiving what we have earned, because we deserve it.

In our earthly work force labor system, if a person is hired and works for another, they are required by law to get payment for that work. The same (work/earnings) law of payment applies in the spiritual realm.

In the realm of the spirit, God has set up a system of payment. God pays in two ways: If you serve Sin - there's judgment; after judgment, the payment is eternal death. But, if you serve God - there are crowns and rewards. The Bible has much to say about these crowns and rewards. When you really look into God's Reward system, it is both brilliant and exciting.

One of the most powerful Christian songs is the "Old Rugged Cross." In one of the stanzas, there are the words that say, *"Until at last, my trophies I lay down. I will cling to the old rugged cross and exchange it someday for a crown."*

For many years, I often wondered what the song writer meant; but, I don't wonder any more because the answer is found in the Word of God.

Just as trophies, rings, and plaques are given to heroes or winning teams in sports and other events, God is going to do the same thing in Heaven. He will be giving out certain types of crowns and rewards for those who were willing to go that extra mile, and willing to give that extra special effort in whatever God had called them to do.

Again, I must emphasize - Salvation cannot be earned or deserved. None of us can ever do enough to afford or merit salvation. Salvation is a Free Gift given for our acceptance of Jesus Christ (by faith) as our personal Savior.

Once we are saved - God expects us to do something with the time we have left on this earth. He expects us to work for Him, for which He has promised payment. Paul says,

"... and every man shall receive his own reward according to his own labor."
I Corinthians 3:8

Each of us must make a personal decision as to how we will live our lives on the Earth. It's either God's way or Our way; God's way gets rewarded.

According to Scripture, there will be Rewards for faithful service for what we do for the Lord (after coming to Christ). God's Word says,

"Therefore, my beloved brethren, be ye stedfast, unmoveable,
always abounding in the work of the Lord,
forasmuch as ye know that your labour is not in vain in the Lord."
I Corinthians 15:58

It's sad, but many believers will meet Christ with a saved soul, but will experience the loss of crowns, and the loss of rewards. The Word of God mentions these losses in the following Scriptures,

"Behold, I come quickly: hold that fast which thou hast,
that no man take thy crown."
Revelation 3:11

"Look to yourselves, that we lose not those things
which we have wrought, but that we receive a full reward."
2 John 1:8

"Every man's work shall be made manifest: for the day shall declare it, because it shall be revealed by fire; and the fire shall try every man's work of what sort it is. If any man's work abide which he hath built thereupon, he shall receive a reward. If any man's work shall be burned, he shall suffer loss: but he himself shall be saved; yet so as by fire."
I Corinthians 3:13-15

In the day of judgment, many believers will feel like shrinking away in shame. Many will see their works burned up. The question on that day will be, "Why did you do - What you did - When you did it?" Was it for God's glory or your glory. The fire will tell.

Bema Seat Judgment

There is a place called the Bema Seat Judgment where only believers will be judged and rewarded.

"For we must all appear before the Judgment Seat of Christ [Bema]; that every one may receive the things done in his body, according to that he hath done, whether it be good or bad."
2 Corinthians 5:10

Bema *[bēma]*= was used to denote a raised place, reached by steps. In the synagogue, the Bema is the raised platform in the center of the synagogue where the Torah is read. One day, the Lord Jesus will be at the Bema to judge our works. This is why we were instructed to,

"Therefore judge nothing before the time, until the Lord come, who both will bring to light the hidden things of darkness, and will make manifest the counsels of the hearts: and then shall every man have praise of God."
I Corinthians 4:5

Believers will be judged, but not for their sins, because their sins were already judged on the cross. But rather, believers are to be judged for the works or faithful service done in their bodies.

Five Crowns

Five types of Crowns are mentioned that will be given to those who are faithful. The meaning of these five crowns is far beyond what we can think or imagine. Nevertheless, in faith, because God requires that we receive these crowns, we are to press toward obtaining them.

Following is a brief explanation concerning the crowns and rewards that God has promised His children who have earned them.

I. Incorruptible Crown - received for personal temperance and self-control.

"Know ye not that they which run in a race run all,
but one receiveth the prize? So run, that ye may obtain.
And every man that striveth for the mastery is temperate in all things.
Now they do it to obtain a corruptible crown; but we an Incorruptible."
I Corinthians 9:24,25

A crown will be given for those who kept themselves in good spiritual shape, by the sacrifices made of denying fleshly desires and bodily appetites, in order to successfully complete the call and mission that God had called for them to do.

II. Crown of Rejoicing - received for soul winning.

"For what is our hope, or joy, or Crown of Rejoicing?
Are not even ye in the presence of our Lord Jesus Christ at His coming?"
I Thessalonians 2:19

A crown will be given to those instrumental in helping to win souls to the Lord. The willingness and the desire to be used by Him to witness to others will also be rewarded.

III. Crown of Righteousness - received for righteous living.

"I have fought a good fight, I have finished my course, I have kept the faith:
Henceforth there is laid up for me a Crown of Righteousness, which
the Lord, the Righteous Judge, shall give me at that day: and not to
me only, but unto all them also that love His appearing."
2 Timothy 4:7,8

A crown will be given to those who strived to live a good, faithful, and righteous life for God, while living here on earth.

IV. Crown of Life - received for patient endurance.

"Blessed is the man that endureth temptation: for when he is tried, he shall receive the Crown of Life, which the Lord hath promised to them that love Him."
James 1:12

"Fear none of those things which thou shalt suffer: behold, the devil shall cast some of you into prison, that ye may be tried; and ye shall have tribulation ten days: be thou faithful unto death, and I will give thee a Crown of Life."
Revelation 2:10

A crown will be given to those who have patiently endured severe hardships of trials and testing's of life on God's behalf. They did not complain, or give up on God. They held on, kept praying, reading His Word, and kept the faith.

V. Crown of Glory - received for feeding the flock of God.

"Feed the flock of God which is among you .... And when the Chief Shepherd shall appear, ye shall receive a Crown of Glory that fadeth not away."
I Peter 5:2,4

A crown will be given to those who faithfully feed the flock of God by preaching, teaching, training, and being an example to others. Since every believer is called to witness in some capacity, this crown is available to all.

Other Rewards

"He that receiveth a prophet in the name of a prophet shall receive a Prophet's Reward; and he that receiveth a righteous man in the name of a righteous man shall receive a Righteous Man's Reward. And whosoever shall give to drink unto one of these little ones a cup of cold water only in the name of a disciple, verily I say unto you, he shall in no wise lose his reward."
Matthew 10:41,42

"Therefore, my beloved brethren, be ye stedfast, unmoveable, always abounding in the work of the Lord, forasmuch as ye know that your labour is not in vain in the Lord."
I Corinthians 15:58

"His lord said unto him, Well done, thou good and faithful servant: thou hast been faithful over a few things, I will make thee ruler over many things: enter thou into the joy of thy lord."
Matthew 25:21

Apostle Paul only cared that his life might be pleasing to Jesus who redeemed him with His precious blood. His desire was to know Jesus more and finish strong. Paul said,

"Not as though I had already attained, either were already perfect: but I follow after, if that I may apprehend that for which also I am apprehended of Christ Jesus."
Philippians 3:12

The Revised Standard Version says,

"Not that I have already obtained this or am already perfect; but I press on to make it my own, because Christ Jesus has made me His own."
Philippians 3:12 RSV

Eternal rewards are ours to obtain. Let's be determined like Paul to press on and follow Christ as he followed Christ!

Remember,

- Salvation is the result of God's work on our behalf.
- Rewards are the result of our work on God's behalf, after coming to Christ.
- Rewards can be lost; salvation cannot.

Test Your Knowledge

*** All answers to the following questions can be found within the pages of this chapter or the Answer Key (at the back of the book).

CHALLENGE YOURSELF: Test your knowledge without referring to the Answer Key

Chapter 20 – Future Rewards

1. We can earn an entrance into Heaven by good works.

   a. True

   b. False

2. Salvation is a ________ ________ given for our acceptance of Jesus Christ (by faith) as our personal Savior.

3. Crowns and rewards can be lost by the believer.

   a. True

   b. False

4. How many types of crowns are mentioned in Scripture that can be earned by believers?

   a. three

   b. six

   c. ten

   d. Five

5. What type of reward is given to one that receives a prophet?

   a. Incorruptible Crown

   b. Prophet's reward

   c. Crown of Life

   d. b and c

6 . What is the name of the Heavenly Court for the righteous (born-again believers)?

   a. The Great White Throne Judgment

   b. The Judgment Seat of Christ

   c. The Bema Seat

   d. b and c

7. God expects us (the believers) to work for Him (not for salvation), for which He has promised payment. Which of the following scripture(s) refer to this statement?

   a. 1 Corinthians 3:8

   b. Luke 20:47

   c. Acts 2:40

   d. Luke 13:27

8. According to Scripture, there will be Rewards for faithful service for what we do for the Lord (after coming to Christ) as stated in I Corinthians 15:58. Which of the following statements is not a part of this scripture?

   a. "… always abounding in the work of the Lord … ."

   b. "… and every man shall receive his own reward according to his own labor"

   c. "Therefore, my beloved brethren, be ye steadfast, unmoveable … ."

   d. "forasmuch as ye know that your labor is not in vain in the Lord"

9. In 2nd John, God warns the believers to "Look to yourselves, that we ___________ not those __________ which we have wrought, but that we receive a _____________________________."

10. Which scripture below talks about the Christian's work being of a certain *sort* and some of those works will be burned, because they will fail the test of possibly ~ Why did you do – What you did – When you did it?

    a. 1 Corinthians 3:13

    b. 1 Corinthians 3:15

    c. 1 Corinthians 3:14

    d. All of the above

11. _______________ was used to denote a raised place, reached by steps. In the synagogue, the _______________ is the raised platform in the center of the synagogue where the Torah is read.

12. In the Heavenly Courtroom, believers will be judged for their sins and for the works and faithful service done in their bodies.

    a. True

    b. False

13. Which Crown will be received for witnessing (encouraging others to invite Jesus into their hearts) and winning souls to Christ?

    a. Crown of Righteousness

    b. Crown of Glory

    c. Crown of Rejoicing

    d. Incorruptible Crown

14. James 1:12 says, "Blessed is the man that ________________________: for when he is tried, he shall receive the Crown of ____________, which the Lord hath promised to them that love Him."

15. Which of the following statements are true?

    a. Salvation is the result of God's work on our behalf.

    b. Rewards are the result of our work on God's behalf, after coming to Christ

    c. Rewards can be lost; Salvation cannot.

    d. All of the above

HOW WELL DID YOU DO?

GRADE SCALE

Missed 0-1 = Excellent
Missed 2 = Very Good
Missed 3 = Good
Missed 4-5 = Average
Mised 6 or more = Need to Re-read Chapter

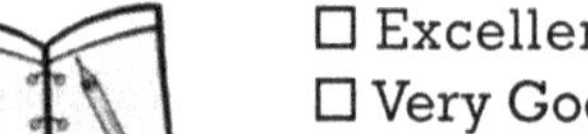

☐ Excellent
☐ Very Good
☐ Good
☐ Average
☐ Need to Re-read Chapter

21

New Heavens & New Earth

The Bible mentions over and over that there are heavens - meaning more than one. The Apostle Paul mentions being caught up to Paradise and calls it *the third Heaven.* If there is a third Heaven, there must be a second and a first heaven. The other heavens can be seen in the following Scriptures.

The first heaven is considered the atmosphere where the birds fly.

"And God said, Let the waters bring forth abundantly the moving creature that hath and fowl that may fly above the earth in the open firmament of heaven."
Genesis 1:20

The second heaven is said to consist of the sun, moon, stars, and the sky which God also created that (daily and constantly) declare His glory, by speaking without words. For example, the sun speaks by rising at one end of the heavens and follows its course to the other end. Nothing can hide from its heat, as stated in the following verses,

"The heavens declare the glory of God; and the firmament sheweth His handywork. Day unto day uttereth speech, and night unto night sheweth knowledge. There is no speech nor language, where their voice is not heard. Their line is gone out through all the earth, and their words to the end of the world. In them hath He set a tabernacle for the sun, Which is as a bridegroom coming out of his chamber, and rejoiceth as a strong man to run a race.

His going forth is from the end of the heaven, and his circuit unto the ends of it: and there is nothing hid from the heat thereof."
Psalm 19:1-6

Interestingly, the Bible says that the current earth is eternal.

"And He built His sanctuary like high palaces, like the earth which He hath established for ever."
Psalm 78:69

The Prophet Isaiah was the first to let us know about God's plan for the current heavens and earth. God said through the Prophet,

"For, behold, I create new heavens and a new earth: and the former shall not be remembered, nor come into mind."
Isaiah 65:17

The Apostle John was given a revelation, whereby, he too saw that the first heaven and the first earth were passed away. Our earth, as we know it now, and our atmospheric heaven, will pass away. John said,

"And I saw a new heaven and a new earth: for the first heaven and the first earth were passed away; and there was no more sea."
Revelation 21:1

The Apostle Peter also talks of the new heavens and a new earth; he said,

"Nevertheless we, according to His promise, look for new heavens and a new earth, wherein dwelleth righteousness."
2 Peter 3:13

How can this be, if the current earth is eternal? Will they both exist? The answer to these questions can be answered by taking a closer look at the word "NEW".

Before we look at the word "new" we must remember that the Apostle Peter let us know, this present world is said to have perished (once before) by water.

"... and the earth standing out of the water and in the water: Whereby the world that then was, being overflowed with water, perished."
2 Peter 3:5,6

The Greek word for "New" = Strong's G2537 - *kainos [kī-no's]* - recently made, fresh, unused.

Vine's Expositor Dictionary says, New - denotes that which is unaccustomed or unused, not new in time, recent, but new as to form or quality, of different nature from what is contrasted as old.

This same word *kainos* is used many times in Scripture. In one example, it is used to describe a person becoming a new man in Christ (new character of manhood, spiritual and moral, after the pattern of Christ), as stated in the following scriptures.

"And that ye put on the new man,
which after God is created in righteousness and true holiness."
Ephesians 4:24

Another example of this word *kainos* is used to describe what happened on the day of Pentecost when it speaks of new tongues. These languages, however, were *new* and *different.* Not in the sense that they had never been heard before, or that they were new to the hearers, for it is plain from verse eight that this is not the case; they were new languages to the speakers, different from those in which they were accustomed to speak.

"... In My name ... they shall speak with new [kainos] tongues ... ."
Mark 16:17

"And they were all filled with the Holy Ghost, and began to speak
with other tongues, as the Spirit gave them utterance."
Acts 2:4

"And how hear we every man in our own tongue, wherein we were born?"
Acts 2:8

Therefore, the promise of new heavens and a new earth points to renewal; not to re-creation. Satan has not won. God will not be forced to start all over again, creating a new heaven and a new earth; because the present heaven and earth will be purged of all that has defiled them. Everything will (again) be made perfect as things were in the Garden of Eden before the Fall.

This renewal process is what Jesus was referring to when He spoke of the regeneration. Jesus said,

"... Verily I say unto you, That ye which have followed Me, in the
regeneration when the Son of man shall sit in the throne of His glory,

ye also shall sit upon twelve thrones, judging the twelve tribes of Israel."
Matthew 19:28

Regeneration = Strongs #3824 - *Paliggenesia - [pä-lēn-ge-ne-sē'-ä]* - new birth, reproduction, renewal.

Strong's Lexicon says this about regeneration, "The word often used to denote the restoration of a thing to its pristine state. The signal and glorious change of all things (in heaven and earth) for the better, that restoration of the primal and perfect condition of things which existed before the fall of our first parents, which the Jews looked for in connection with the advent of the Messiah, and which Christians expected in connection with the visible return of Jesus from Heaven."

In the book of Acts, Regeneration is similar to Apostle Peter's reference concerning (this same renewal) when he spoke about "the times of restitution" on the Day of Pentecost.

"And He shall send Jesus Christ, which before was
preached unto you: Whom the Heaven must receive
until the times of restitution of all things, which God hath
spoken by the mouth of all His holy prophets since the world began."
Acts 3:20,21

To further clarify the similarity of the meaning of regeneration and restitution, let's look at the definition of restitution.

Restitution = Strong's #605 – *apokatastasis - [ä-po-kä-tä'-stä-sēs]* - restoration; of the perfect state before the Fall.

Prior to the restoration of the Earth, the Apostle Peter lets us know how God will purge this earth.

"But the heavens and the earth, which are now, by the same word
are kept in store, reserved unto fire against the day of judgment ... .

... in the which the heavens shall pass away with a great noise,
and the elements shall melt with fervent heat, the earth also
and the works that are therein shall be burned up.

... the heavens being on fire shall be dissolved,
and the elements shall melt with fervent heat?"
2 Peter 3:7,10,12

Out of the old will come the new. From Scripture, we see that the new purified earth will no longer have a sea.

"And I saw a new heaven and a new earth: for the first heaven and the first earth were passed away; and there was no more sea."
Revelation 21:1

We are told that water covers about 3/5 of the earth's surface. Without the sea, there will be much more land space for people to live in the New Earth. The whole earth will become habitable. Jesus said,

"Blessed are the meek: for they shall inherit the earth."
Matthew 5:5

The Apostle Paul spoke of the time when the creation shall experience its deliverance from the bondage of corruption which it was subjected to because of Adam's sin. After Adam sinned (disobeyed God) in the Garden of Eden; God made the following statement,

"And unto Adam He said ... cursed is the ground for thy sake; ...
Thorns also and thistles shall it bring forth to thee .... ."
Genesis 3:17,18

"For we know that the whole creation groaneth
and travaileth in pain together until now .... ."
Romans 8:22

The new Heavens and the new Earth are going to be far beyond anything that our imagination can even begin to conjure up. Somehow (the renewed) new heavens and new earth are destined to play a permanent part in the future of the people of God.

Currently, we have partial vision and partial knowledge of what God has in store for us within this new heavenly environment. Those things are without earthly example, above human experience, and beyond our wildest imaginations. The Word of God states,

"But as it is written, Eye hath not seen, nor ear heard,
neither have entered into the heart of man,
the things which God hath prepared for them that love Him."
I Corinthians 2:9

All we have in this life is a foretaste and snapshot of the great and glorious things that God has chosen to reveal to us concerning the things to come.

There are many activities that will take place during the Millennium (1,000 year reign of Christ). Isaiah gives us a snapshot of a glorious future on earth, where man and beast will live together in peace as seen in the following scriptures.

"The wolf also shall dwell with the lamb,
and the leopard shall lie down with the kid;
and the calf and the young lion and the fatling together;
and a little child shall lead them.

And the cow and the bear shall feed;
their young ones shall lie down together:
and the lion shall eat straw like the ox.

And the sucking child shall play on the hole of the asp [cobra],
and the weaned child shall put his hand on the cockatrice [viper's] den.
They shall not hurt nor destroy in all My holy mountain:
for the earth shall be full of the knowledge of the LORD,
as the waters cover the sea."
Isaiah 11:6-9

"... and they shall beat their swords into plowshares,
and their spears into pruning hooks: nation shall not lift up
sword against nation, neither shall they learn war any more."
Isaiah 2:4

After the 1,000 year time period, the activities of the Millennium may or may not carry over to the new earth.

Therefore, we are concentrating on what the Scripture has to say about the eternal ages of ages, after the Millennium. Regardless, whatever God has in store for the new heavens and the new earth, it will be incredible.

"The secret things belong unto the LORD our God .... "
Deuteronomy 29:29

"... unto Him that is able to do
exceeding abundantly above all that we ask or think .... "
Ephesians 3:20

Praise God, we believers will be there to share in it all.

❖

Test Your Knowledge

*** All answers to the following questions can be found within the pages of this chapter or the Answer Key (at the back of the book).

CHALLENGE YOURSELF: Test your knowledge without referring to the Answer Key

Chapter 21 – New Heavens & New Earth

1. According to Scripture, there is more than one heaven that is mentioned.
   a. True
   b. False

2. Isaiah tells us that the present heavens and earth will not be ___________, nor come into ______________.

3. The Greek word *kainos* means:
   a. Used
   b. of different nature from what is contrasted as old
   c. brand new - never ever existed before
   d. having great knowledge

4. The Greek word for Regeneration is:
   a. pamplēthei
   b. rhēma
   c. paliggenesia
   d. Parepidēmos

5. The Bible mentions a time period of peace whereby the leopard shall lie down with the kid (goat). This time period is called:

    a. Tribulation

    b. Rapture

    c. Great White Throne

    d. Millennium

6. We only have partial vision and partial knowledge of what God has in store for us within the new heavenly environment.

    a. True

    b. False

7. The Greek word *apokatastasis* is translated as:

    a. Forgiveness

    b. Sacrifice

    c. Restitution

    d. Apology

8. The ________________ heaven is said to consist of the sun, moon, stars, and the sky which God also ______________________ that daily declare His glory by ____.

9. The ________________ heaven is considered the atmosphere where the birds fly.

10. Which scripture below talks about the heaven in question #9.

a. Genesis 1:25

b. Genesis 2:9

c. Genesis 1:20

d. Genesis 2:23

11. The promise of new heavens and a new earth points to renewal. This renewal process is what Jesus was referring to when He spoke of the ______________________ in Matthew chapter 19.

12. Strong's Lexicon says this about ______________________, the word often used to denote *the restoration of a thing to its pristine state.*

13. Which scripture(s) lets us know how God will purge this Earth?

    a. 2 Corinthians 5:10

    b. 1 Corinthians 4:5

    c. 2 Peter 3:7,10,12

    d. a and b

14. From Scripture, we see that the new purified earth will no longer have a sea.

    a. True

    b. False

15. All we (Believer's) have in this life is a ___________________ and ____________________ of the great and glorious things that God has chosen to reveal to us concerning the things to come in the Afterlife.

GRADE SCALE

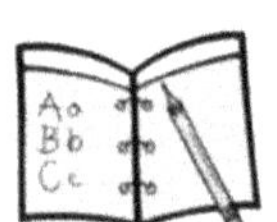

Missed 0-1 = Excellent
Missed 2 = Very Good
Missed 3 = Good
Missed 4-5 = Average
Mised 6 or more = Need to Re-read Chapter

HOW WELL DID YOU DO?

- ☐ Excellent
- ☐ Very Good
- ☐ Good
- ☐ Average
- ☐ Need to Re-read Chapter

22

The New Jerusalem

We must keep in mind that when the Scriptures speak of the new heavens, it is not talking about a re-creation of the third Heaven which is the habitation of God. Nowhere, does the Bible suggest that there is anything abnormal or requires the renewal of God's dwelling place.

The Heaven of Heavens

The Heaven of heavens is a definite place.

"Thou, even thou, art LORD alone; Thou hast made Heaven, the Heaven of heavens, with all their host, the earth, and all things that are therein, the seas, and all that is therein, and thou preservest them all; and the host of Heaven worshippeth thee."
Nehemiah 9:6

Heaven is the region spoken of as the immediate presence where God dwells; also, the dwelling place of angels and saints. Evidently it is above, because Jesus looked up as He lifted His eyes to call on His Father.

"These words spake Jesus, and lifted up His eyes to Heaven, and said, Father, the hour is come; glorify Thy Son, that Thy Son also may glorify Thee."
John 17:1

"... and hear Thou in Heaven Thy dwelling place ... ."
I Kings 8:30

"The LORD is in His holy temple, the LORD'S throne is in Heaven ... ."
Psalm 11:4

Jesus referred to Heaven as "My Father's House." He spoke of going and preparing an infinitely more exciting and rewarding life of unimaginable blessings.

"In my Father's house are many mansions .... I go to prepare a place for you. And if I go and prepare a place for you, I will come again, and receive you unto Myself; that where I am, there ye may be also."
John 14:2,3

"But as it is written, Eye hath not seen, nor ear heard, neither have entered into the heart of man, the things which God hath prepared for them that love Him."
I Corinthians 2:9

The Apostle Paul called this place the Third Heaven and also Paradise.

"I knew a man in Christ above fourteen years ago ... such an one caught up to the third Heaven. And I knew such a man ... How that he was caught up into Paradise, and heard unspeakable words, which it is not lawful for a man to utter."
2 Corinthians 12:2-4

Paul let us know that human language cannot illustrate the glories of Heaven. These stories far outweigh the most magnificent description ever given by man. Out of all that we have read, heard, and dreamed about Heaven, (one day) we shall say as the Queen of Sheba said to Solomon,

"... until I came, and mine eyes had seen it: and, behold, the half was not told me: thy wisdom and prosperity exceedeth the fame which I heard."
I Kings 10:7

The glories of Heaven are so magnificent, Jesus prayed that we would be kept, to ensure we would be with Him on the other side; to see the glory that He has with the Father. Jesus said,

"Father, I will that they also, whom Thou hast given Me, be with Me where I am; that they may behold My glory, which thou hast given Me .... "
John 17:24

Jesus gave the Apostle John a foretaste of what's going on around God's throne. One day, we believers will join this heavenly throng in worship and praise to the Lamb of God - the Lord Jesus Christ.

"And I beheld, and I heard the voice of many angels round about the throne and the beasts and the elders: and the number of them was ten thousand times ten thousand, and thousands of thousands; Saying with a loud voice, Worthy is the Lamb that was slain to receive power, and riches, and wisdom, and strength, and honour, and glory, and blessing."
Revelation 5:11,12

Apostle Paul also had a glimpse of the foretaste of God's glory, as he looked forward to going immediately into the presence of Christ, he said,

"For to me to live is Christ, and to die is gain."
Philippians 1:21

"For I reckon that the sufferings of this present time are not worthy to be compared with the glory which shall be revealed in us."
Romans 8:18

For the believer, the best is yet to come. I'm sure we'll be amazed at what awaits us on the other side. God hasn't revealed even a fraction of what He has in mind for us.

"That in the ages to come He might shew the exceeding riches of His grace in His kindness toward us through Christ Jesus."
Ephesians 2:7

As we look forward to going to our new home (Heaven) in Scripture, we see spiritual concepts and promises in a vague outline as if we are looking through steamed glass. Someday, we will see clearly. Apostle Paul said,

"For now we see through a glass, darkly; but then face to face: now I know in part; but then shall I know even as also I am known."
I Corinthians 13:12

God assures us that His promise of eternal life is more than worth the effort, struggles, and disappointments of life and death. Paul said,

"For our light affliction, which is but for a moment, worketh for us a far more exceeding and eternal weight of glory."
2 Corinthians 4:17

The New Jerusalem

Scripture mentions a place called the New Jerusalem. New Jerusalem is described as a magnificent kingdom with a magnificent beauty that we cannot comprehend.

The New Jerusalem is the city where God abides, which will descend directly from Heaven, according to the following Scriptures,

"... which is New Jerusalem,
which cometh down out of Heaven from my God ... ."
Revelation 3:12

"... and showed me that great city, the Holy Jerusalem,
descending out of Heaven from God, Having the glory of God ... ."
Revelation 21:10

Scripture never says this city touches the earth. It seems to be suspended in mid-air above the new earth.

This city will be like a square or cube. Its size will be 12,000 furlongs. Vine's Expository Dictionary says, a furlong [stadion] is 600 Greek feet, or 1/8 of a Roman mile. Bible Scholars believe this city may literally be 1,400 to 1,500 miles in circumference, with its length to be as great as its width.

"And he that talked with me had a golden reed to measure the city,
and the gates thereof, and the wall thereof. And the city lieth foursquare,
and the length is as large as the breadth: and he measured the city
with the reed, twelve thousand furlongs. The length and
the breadth and the height of it are equal.

And he measured the wall thereof, an hundred and forty and four cubits,
according to the measure of a man, that is, of the angel. And the building of
the wall of it was of jasper: and the city was pure gold, like unto clear glass."
Revelation 21:15-18

The New Living Translation quotes these verses by saying,

"The angel who talked to me held in his hand a gold measuring stick
to measure the city, its gates, and its wall. When he measured it,
he found it was a square, as wide as it was long.

In fact, it's length and width and height were each 1,400 miles.

Then he measured the walls and found them to be 216 feet thick
(according to the human standard used by the angel).
The wall was made of jasper, and the city was pure gold, as clear as glass."
Revelation 21:15-18 NLT

John lets us know that the thick walls of the celestial, chandelier type city of pure gold, shines brilliantly as clear as glass. What a sight it must be to see these miles of jasper reflected on the golden streets of the city.

God's Presence in The New Jerusalem

Scripture lets us know that the Throne of God the Father and God the Son, is located in the New Jerusalem.

"And I John saw the holy city, New Jerusalem, coming down from God out of Heaven ... And I heard a great voice out of Heaven saying, Behold, the tabernacle of God is with men, and He will dwell with them, and they shall be His people, and God Himself shall be with them, and be their God."
Revelation 21:2,3

"And I saw the holy city, the new Jerusalem, coming down from God out of Heaven ... I heard a loud shout from the throne, saying, Look, God's home is now among His people! He will live with them, and they will be His people. God Himself will be with them."
Revelation 21:2,3 NLT

"And I saw no temple therein:
for the Lord God Almighty and the Lamb are the temple of it."
Revelation 21:22

The Gates of New Jerusalem

The gates surrounding the city were described as being made of pearls. John says this of the New Jerusalem,

"And had a wall great and high, and had twelve gates,
and at the gates twelve angels, and names written thereon,
which are the names of the twelve tribes of the children of Israel:

On the east three gates; on the north three gates;
on the south three gates; and on the west three gates."
Revelation 21:12,13

"And the twelve gates were twelve pearls;
every several gate was of one pearl:
and the street of the city was pure gold, as it were transparent glass."
Revelation 21:21

"And the gates of it shall not be shut at all by day:
for there shall be no night there."
Revelation 21:25

The Foundations of New Jerusalem

The foundations of the New Jerusalem far exceeds out finite imagination. The magnificent description is as follows.

"And the wall of the city had twelve foundations,
and in them the names of the twelve apostles of the Lamb."
Revelation 21:14

"And the foundations of the wall of the city were garnished with all manner of precious stones. The first foundation was jasper; the second, sapphire; the third, a chalcedony; the fourth, an emerald; The fifth, sardonyx; the sixth, sardius; the seventh, chrysolite; the eighth, beryl; the ninth, a topaz; the tenth, a chrysoprasus; the eleventh, a jacinth; the twelfth, an amethyst."
Revelation 21:19,20

The New Jerusalem is a real place where people with physical, glorified bodies will dwell in God's presence for all eternity. Because of what Jesus Christ accomplished on our behalf, the New Jerusalem belongs to those who believe on His Name. The Apostles Paul and Peter make two awesome statements concerning our future inheritance. They said,

"And if children, then heirs; heirs of God, and joint-heirs with Christ;
if so be that we suffer with Him, that we may be also glorified together."
Romans 8:17

"To an inheritance incorruptible, and undefiled,
and that fadeth not away, reserved in Heaven for you."
I Peter 1:4

What Will The New Jerusalem Be Like?

In the New Jerusalem, there will be (both) the conscious presence of God and the sight of Jesus Christ. Throughout all eternity, we will have the privilege of basking in His radiance.

On the Damascus road, Saul of Tarsus saw a vision of Jesus Christ, which was a light brighter than the noon day sun that blinded him for three days. Born-again believers, in our new glorified state, will be able to look at Jesus and not be affected by His radiance. John said,

"And they shall see His face ... ."
Revelation 22:4

"... and He will dwell with them, and they shall be His people,
and God Himself shall be with them, and be their God."
Revelation 21:3

On that day, the whole family (Old and New Testament saints) will be there.

"... the whole family in Heaven ... ."
Ephesians 3:15

"And the city had no need of the sun, neither of the moon,
to shine in it: for the glory of God did lighten it,
and the Lamb is the light thereof."
Revelation 21:23

"And there shall be no night there;
and they need no candle,
neither light of the sun;
for the Lord God giveth them light:
and they shall reign for ever and ever."
Revelation 22:5

"And the gates of it shall not be shut at all by day ... ."
Revelation 21:25

"And God shall wipe away all tears from their eyes;
and there shall be no more death, neither sorrow, nor crying,
neither shall there be any more pain:
for the former things are passed away."
Revelation 21:4

"They shall hunger no more, neither thirst any more;
neither shall the sun light on them, nor any heat."
Revelation 7:16

What 'Will Not' Be In The New Jerusalem?

Only that which is righteous and holy will be able to enter into the Holy City. God says,

"And there shall in no wise enter into it anything that defileth,
neither whatsoever worketh abomination, or maketh a lie:
but they which are written in the Lamb's Book of Life."
Revelation 21:27

"For without are dogs, and sorcerers, and whoremongers,
and murderers, and idolaters, and whosoever loveth and maketh a lie."
Revelation 22:15

What Will We Be Doing Throughout All Eternity?

I dare not speculate – but there will be no boredom or idleness there. The scriptures that speak of our eternity with Him are beyond our comprehension. This is where others have pressed on, walked by faith, and so should we. If God said it, it shall be so. The Apostle John wrote,

"... that they may rest from their labours ... ."
Revelation 14:13

The Bible does not go into detail as to what our activities will be in the eternal state. It simply says that we will serve God. Whatever it is, it will be a meaningful and fulfilling service.

"Therefore are they before the throne of God,
and serve Him day and night in His temple ... ."
Revelation 7:15

"To him that overcometh will I grant to sit with Me in My throne,
even as I also overcame, and am set down with My Father in His throne."
Revelation 3:21

"Him that overcometh will I make a pillar in the temple of My God ... ."
Revelation 3:12

"... and they shall walk with Me in white: for they are worthy."
Revelation 3:4

"He that overcometh, the same shall be clothed in white raiment .... "
Revelation 3:5

"... Unto Him that loved us, and washed us from our sins in His own blood,
And hath made us kings and priests unto God and His Father .... "
Revelation 1:5,6

"Know ye not that we shall judge angels? .... "
I Corinthians 6:3

"His lord said unto him, Well done, thou good and faithful servant:
thou hast been faithful over a few things, I will make thee
ruler over many things: enter thou into the joy of thy lord."
Matthew 25:21

Will We Know Each Other In The New Jerusalem?

The New Testament seems to indicate that our identities will remain unchanged in our new glorified state. Personally, I don't believe that we will be nameless, faceless individuals without an identity.

I say this because, in the underworld of Hades, the rich man through divine revelation recognized Abraham who had died hundreds of years earlier. The rich man also saw and recognized Lazarus.

"And in Hell [Hades] he lift up his eyes ...
and seeth Abraham afar off, and Lazarus in his bosom [Paradise]."
Luke 16:23

I believe it will be the same in Heaven.

Moses and Elijah suddenly appeared with Christ on the Mount of Transfiguration. Even though they had died centuries before, they still maintained a clear identity. Through a divine revelation, Peter, James, and John, recognized them and knew who they were.

"And, behold, there appeared unto them Moses and Elias talking with Him.
Then answered Peter, and said unto Jesus, Lord, it is good for us to be here:
if thou wilt, let us make here three tabernacles; one for Thee,
and one for Moses, and one for Elias."
Matthew 17:3,4

This implies that in our perfected form, we will somehow be able to recognize people we've never even seen before. Jesus said,

"... many shall come from the east and west, and shall sit down with Abraham, and Isaac, and Jacob, in the Kingdom of Heaven."
Matthew 8:11

We will be able to have fellowship with Adam, Eve, Enoch, Noah, Abraham, Jacob, Samuel, Moses, Joshua, Esther, Elijah, Elisha, Isaiah, Daniel, Ezekiel, David, Peter, Barnabas, Paul, any of the saints, and our loved ones. For that to be possible, we must *all* retain our individual identities and not *all* turn into common generic beings.

Jesus, who is our example was recognizable after His resurrection. Mary and the disciples recognized Him.

"Jesus saith unto her, Mary. She turned herself, and saith unto Him, Rabboni; which is to say, Master."
John 20:16

"And their eyes were opened, and they knew Him; and He vanished out of their sight."
Luke 24:31

The Apostle Paul when speaking about physical death and the sorrow that it brings on this side, spoke words to comfort our hearts by saying, that we shall see our born-again loved ones again. Paul said,

"... and the dead in Christ shall rise first: Then we which are alive and remain shall be caught up together with them in the clouds, to meet the Lord in the air: and so shall we ever be with the Lord. Wherefore comfort one another with these words."
I Thessalonians 4:16-18

The prospect of reunion brings comfort. There would be little comfort (in the reunion) if we could not recognize one another.

There won't be anyone in Heaven that Jesus does not know. Through divine revelation, I believe that we shall know each other also. John said,

"... when He shall appear, we shall be like Him ... ."
I John 3:2

Paul speaks of this increase of divine knowledge we will have when we are with the Lord Jesus Christ, by saying,

"For now we see through a glass, darkly; but then face to face: now I know in part; but then shall I know even as also I am known."
I Corinthians 13:12

In Heaven, people from all of history, from every nation, race, and tongue, will be there; we will be one big happy family. The size of the family will not matter in the infinite perfection of Heaven. There will be plenty of time for unending fellowship with everyone.

The song says, "When we all get to Heaven, what a day of rejoicing that will be. When we all see Jesus, we will sing and shout the victory." Hallelujah!

Will There Be Eating and Drinking In The New Jerusalem?

In our new resurrected, glorified bodies, the physical appetite for food will not be as we know it now.

In this life, we are under the power of bodily appetites, with the desire for food and drink being major for survival. In the next life, we don't seem to be under the power of these bodily appetites, even though eating and drinking will be done.

In the Gospel of Luke, we see Jesus eating, even though He had a resurrected glorified body.

"And when He had thus spoken, He shewed them His hands and His feet. And while they yet believed not for joy, and wondered, He said unto them, Have ye here any meat? And they gave Him a piece of a broiled fish, and of an honeycomb. And He took it, and did eat before them."
Luke 24:40-43

Even though we see Jesus in this passage eating a piece of broiled fish, Paul speaks of God one day destroying the act of meat eating. He says,

"Meats for the belly, and the belly for meats: but God shall destroy both it and them. ... ."
I Corinthians 6:13

In scripture, we are not told all of the intricate details of our new glorified bodies, but we must remember that in the Garden of Eden, Adam and Eve were not meat eaters. Even during the 1,000 year reign of Christ (Millennium) the Scriptures speaks of the nature of animals being changed.

"And the cow and the bear shall feed; their young ones shall lie down together: and the lion shall eat straw like the ox."
Isaiah 11:7

"The wolf and the lamb shall feed together, and the lion shall eat straw like the bullock: and dust shall be the serpent's meat. They shall not hurt nor destroy in all My holy mountain, saith the LORD."
Isaiah 65:25

While sharing the Passover meal with His disciples, Christ promised that He would drink the fruit of the vine together with them again in Heaven. Jesus said,

"... Take this, and divide it among yourselves; For I say unto you, I will not drink of the fruit of the vine, until the kingdom of God shall come."
Luke 22:17-18

"... I will not drink henceforth of this fruit of the vine, until that day when I drink it new with you in My Father's kingdom."
Matthew 26:29

"For I say unto you, I will not any more eat thereof, until it be fulfilled in the Kingdom of God."
Luke 22:16

"That ye may eat and drink at My table in My Kingdom .... ."
Luke 22:30

"... To him that overcometh will I give to eat of the Tree of Life, which is in the midst of the Paradise of God."
Revelation 2:7

"... To him that overcometh will I give to eat of the hidden manna .... ."
Revelation 2:17

What joy it's going to be to dine and fellowship with JESUS and all the other saints of God at the Heavenly feast in the New Jerusalem that shall never cease. You don't want to miss it!

Will There Be Marriage and Sex In The New Jerusalem?

In Heaven, the bodily appetite for sex will be gone forever. We will not marry, but we will be like the angels. When asked about future martial relationships, Jesus spoke these words,

"And Jesus answering said unto them, The children of this world marry, and are given in marriage: But they which shall be accounted worthy to obtain that world, and the resurrection from the dead, neither marry, nor are given in marriage: Neither can they die any more: for they are equal unto the angels; and are the children of God, being the children of the resurrection."
Luke 20:34-36

The only marriage in Heaven will be our relationship to the Lord Jesus Christ. We, the body of Christ, are also the bride of Christ and will be married to the Lamb. The Apostle Paul spoke this mystery over and over again, by saying,

"This is a great mystery: but I speak concerning Christ and the Church."
Ephesians 5:32

"For I am jealous over you with godly jealousy: for I have espoused you to one husband, that I may present you as a chaste virgin to Christ."
2 Corinthians 11:2

"Let us be glad and rejoice, and give honour to Him: for the marriage of the Lamb is come, and His wife [body of Christ] hath made herself ready."
Revelation 19:7

"Husbands, love your wives, even as Christ also loved the Church, and gave Himself for it; That he might sanctify and cleanse it with the washing of water by the word, That He might present it to Himself a glorious church, not having spot, or wrinkle, or any such thing; but that it should be holy and without blemish."
Ephesians 5:25-27

In Heaven, in the place of sex, there will be many other unimaginable, unspoken pleasures (for evermore) that God has in store for us.

"They shall be abundantly satisfied with the fatness of Thy house; and thou shalt make them drink of the river of Thy pleasures."
Psalm 36:8

"Thou wilt shew me the path of life: in Thy presence is fulness of joy; at Thy right hand there are pleasures for evermore."
Psalm 16:11

Take note that the scriptures quoted above, speak of God's river of pleasures and His pleasures for evermore. The pleasures of sin (with all of it's ungodly lusts) which have captivated those in this present world, are only for a season. None of this world's sinful pleasures can tap or compare to what we will experience throughout all eternity.

On the Cross Jesus said,

"... It is finished ... ."
John 19:30

Jesus finished His work on Earth, so that our eternity with Him will never be finished; it will never end.

Have you ever watched a movie so good, you wished it would never end? Have you ever savored a dessert so sweet, you wished it would last and last? Have you had a relationship so fulfilling, you hoped it would go on forever?

Eternal life with God will be so much better. It enhances all of the positives - love, joy, peace, and happiness; while eliminating all of the negatives - sinful lusts, stresses, wants, needs, greed, envy, or any other vices.

God loves and desires only the best for us (now) and in eternity. If you're worried about feeling out of place in Heaven, don't. It's the earth (here and now) whereby, we are strangers and pilgrims. Heaven is our home. It has been prepared by Jesus to be the place where we will live together and enjoy Him forever in the fullness of our glorified humanity.

"Beloved, now are we the sons of God, and it doth not yet appear what we shall be: but we know that, when He shall appear, we shall be like Him; for we shall see Him as He is."
I John 3:2

Is it any wonder that the psalmist said,

"Precious in the sight of the Lord is the death of His saints?"
Psalm 116:15

In the ages to come, God will show us more and more of His great grace and glory. Wow - the best is yet to come.

The Apostle Paul speaks of the glories of the eternal ages, by saying,

"That in the ages to come He might shew the exceeding riches of His grace in His kindness toward us through Christ Jesus."
Ephesians 2:7

Eternity With Jesus

The Light of Heaven is the *face* of Jesus;
The Joy of Heaven is the *presence* of Jesus;
The Melody of Heaven is the *name* of Jesus;
The Harmony of Heaven is the *praise* of Jesus;
The Theme of Heaven is the *work* of Jesus;
The Employment of Heaven is the *service* of Jesus;
The Fullness of Heaven is *Jesus* Himself. Author Unknown

Test Your Knowledge

*** All answers to the following questions can be found within the pages of this chapter or the Answer Key (at the back of the book).

CHALLENGE YOURSELF: Test your knowledge without referring to the Answer Key

Chapter 22 – The New Jerusalem

1. Paul said that in the ________ to come, God will show the __________ __________ of His grace and kindness toward us through Christ Jesus.

2. The New Jerusalem has how many pearly gates:
   a. 24
   b. 7
   c. 12
   d. 3

3. The size of the city (the New Jerusalem) will be how many furlongs?
   a. 1,500
   b. 600
   c. 1,400
   d. 12,000

4. In the New Jerusalem, there will only be *Night* every now and then.
   a. True
   b. False

5. Jesus specifically mentions three Old Testament patriarchs that many will sit down with in the New Jerusalem. Who are they?

   a. Abraham, Issachar, Jacob

   b. Jacob, Abraham, Isaac

   c. Adam, Isaac, Jacob

   d. Abraham, Isaac, Joseph

6. In God's ___________ there is fullness of __________; and at His right hand there are ____________ for evermore.

7. In reference to question #3, if a furlong is equivalent to approximately 1/8 of a Roman mile, what is the approximate circumstance (length, width, and height) of the Holy City (the New Jerusalem)?

   a. 500 to 600 miles

   b. 800 to 1000 miles

   c. 1100 to 1200 miles

   d. 1400 to 1500 miles

8. According to the human standard used by the angel, how thick were the walls of the celestial chandelier type city of pure gold, which shined brightly as clear as glass?

   a. 216 feet

   b. 132 feet

   c. 144 feet

   d. 96 feet

9. The Heaven of heavens is a definite place and is the region spoken of as the immediate presence where God dwells; also, the dwelling place of the Angels and Born-Again Believers. Which of the following scriptures speak of the Heaven of heavens?

   a. Deuteronomy 10:14

   b. 1 Kings 8:30

   c. Psalm 11:4

   d. 2 Corinthians 12:2-4

   e. All of the above

10. Jesus referred to Heaven as ______________________________. He spoke of going and preparing an infinitely more exciting and rewarding life of ______________________ blessings.

11. 2 Corinthians chapter _______ verse ______ assures us that God's promise of Eternal Life is more than worth the effort, struggles, and disappointments of life and death.

12. The New Jerusalem where God abides, will come down out of Heaven according to which scripture below?

    a. Revelation 21:15-18

    b. Revelation 3:12

    c. Revelation 21:10

    d. Revelation 21:2,3

    e. b, c, and d

    f. All of the above

13. There will be a temple in the New Jerusalem.

    a. True

    b. False

14. The New Jerusalem is a real place where people with ___________ __________________________ will dwell in God presence for all eternity.

15. In Romans 8 verse _____ and 1 Peter 1 verse _____, the Apostles (Paul and Peter) make two awesome statements concerning our future state (inheritance).

16. The wall of the city (the New Jerusalem) had how many foundations?

    a. 24

    b. 7

    c. 12

    d. 3

17. Which of the following is not a precious stone used in the foundations of question #16?

    a. Jasper, Sapphire, Chalcedony, Emerald

    b. Sardonyx, Sardius, Chrysolite (peridot), Beryl

    c. Garnet, Jade, Peruvian Opal, Coral

    d. Topaz, Chrysoprasus (chrysoprase), Jacinth, Amethyst

18. According to Revelation 21:25, in our new glorified state, we will be able to look at Jesus and not be affected by His radiance.

    a. True

    b. False

19. Only that which is righteous and holy will be able to enter into the Holy City (the New Jerusalem).

    a. True

    b. False

20. In reference to what we will be doing throughout all eternity, which scripture listed below does not apply?

    a. Revelation 21:15-18

    b. Revelation 3:21

    c. Revelation 14:13

    d. Revelation 7:15

    e. Revelation 1:5,6

    f. b and c

21. In the Afterlife, will we not be nameless, faceless individuals in our new glorified state.

    a. True

    b. False

22. In our new resurrected, ______________________________, the physical _______________ for food will ____________ as we know it now.

23. When asked about marriage in Heaven, Luke 20:34-36 says, "And Jesus answering said unto them, The children of this world ____________, and are given ______________________: But they which shall be accounted worthy to obtain that world, and the resurrection from the dead, ________________________, nor or given _________________: Neither can they ________ any more: for they are equal unto _______________; and are the children of God, being the children of the resurrection."

24. None of the world's _____________________________ pleasures can _________________ to what we will experience throughout all Eternity.

25. In John 19:30, Jesus said, "… It is _____________________."

HOW WELL DID YOU DO?

GRADE SCALE

Missed 0-2 = Excellent
Missed 3-4 = Very Good
Missed 5-6 = Good
Missed 7 = Average
Mised 8 or more = Need to Re-read Chapter

☐ Excellent
☐ Very Good
☐ Good
☐ Average
☐ Need to Re-read Chapter

23

Conclusion

Curiosity about death and the afterlife cannot be silenced, quenched, or ignored. The fact of death must be faced, because it constantly intrudes the circles of our friends and loved ones.

Learning more about death and what happens after death can give priceless comfort and hope in the face of death. This knowledge is powerful and should have a great impact on the kind of person we become. It should help motivate us to live carefully; making wise choices as we prepare to meet God and enter into the eternal life He has offered us.

It's in this life that we are to prepare for the next life. How sad that many people are unprepared and don't take advantage of all God has provided.

"And this is the record, that God hath given
to us eternal life, and this life is in His Son."
I John 5:11

Our earthly lives are only *temporal* compared to eternity. How sad, that many would rather trade the temporal for the eternal by continually enjoying the pleasures of sin, which are only for a moment, rather than accept eternal life in Christ.

"... For what is your life? It is even a vapour,
that appeareth for a little time, and then vanisheth away."
James 4:14

Knowing that the purpose of this life is to prepare us for an eternal life of power and ability beyond anything we can imagine, it should encourage us to turn to God so He can begin to fulfill His purpose in us.

Concerning death and the afterlife, are you believing what you want to believe or are you believing what the evidence shows to be true?

Through the power of the Holy Spirit, much prayer, study, and meditation, I have dug (deep) to make available this Biblical light on death and the afterlife.

Through the simplicity of the Word of God, by the preponderance of the evidence, I believe I have proven my case that physical death is not the end and that there is consciousness after death. Let's strive to be like the Bereans, as they listened to the teachings of the Apostle Paul.

"These were more noble than those in Thessalonica,
in that they received the Word with all readiness of mind,
and searched the scriptures daily, whether those things were so."
Acts 17:11

Read this book carefully, search the scriptures for yourself, pray about it, and meditate on these things. Then, you decide if they are so.

We have a choice where we spend eternity – Heaven (with God) or Hell (without God). Nothing is worth going to Hell, for an eternity.

Jesus Christ said,

"For what shall it profit a man, if he shall gain the whole world,
and lose his own soul? Or what shall a man give in exchange for his soul?"
Mark 8:36

There is only one way to escape the wrath to come. It's through a personal relationship with Jesus Christ. Life's worst mistake is to die without Christ.

After we receive Jesus as Savior, let's prove that He lives within us by showing the new life that He promises and provides.

"Therefore if any man be in Christ, he is a new creature:
old things are passed away; behold, all things are become new."
2 Corinthians 5:17

Salvation is a gift and it's solely by grace. We prove and show that we are truly saved by the works that follow our profession of salvation. Without the fruits of righteousness on daily display in our lives before an unbelieving world, our internal change is questionable.

Let's live for Christ alone, striving to please Him in every act we do. Let's continue to cry out to Him to help us keep our motives clean, our thoughts pure, and our minds heavenly. Let's strive to never be pleased with that which does not please God. But let's follow His every step. Let's obey His every word and be determined to walk in holiness; without sinning.

Let us never forget the things that bring Heavenly rewards:

- Sharing the faith
- Making disciples
- Feeding the hungry
- Clothing the naked
- Praying for the sick
- Visiting those in prison
- Looking after the fatherless and widows

These are just a few of the things that please God. Let's allow these things be *active* in our lives. Everything that we do for Him will not be in vain.

"... forasmuch as ye know, your labor is not in vain in the Lord."
I Corinthians 15:58

While the thought of death and dying may be difficult, we must remember that death cannot separate us (even for a moment) from the love of God, which is in Christ Jesus our Lord.

It was sin that brought death into the world. The supreme sentence of death on sinners have been borne by Jesus. Because of our Substitute – the Lord Jesus Christ - death does not need to be an ultimate end or a final good-bye.

When our appointed time comes and God says, "your time on earth is done"; we are to cling to the Lord Jesus, giving Him all the fears concerning our passing or transitioning from this life to the next. We will not be alone. He will be with us.

Jesus Christ - He is our consolation. We must give the end of our earthly lives to Him, praying:

"... Father, into Thy hands I commend my spirit ... ."
Luke 23:46

For believers, the hour of death becomes a transition that initiates a new phase of life that leads us from the earthly - to the Heavenly, to be with our precious Lord.

Also, for believers, Jesus fulfills His own promise when He said,

"... I will come again, and receive you unto Myself;
that where I am, there ye may be also."
John 14:3

Remember: Whatever we suffer in this life, cannot be compared with the glory of the life to come. When our earthly journey ends, our eternal journey is only beginning.

"If ye then be risen with Christ, seek those things which are above,
where Christ sitteth on the right hand of God.
Set your affection on things above, not on things on the earth."
Colossians 3:1,2

I pray the Holy Spirit sends the urgent message of this book (home) to the heart of every believer and unbeliever.

God bless you!

24

Invitation

Hell is not a pleasant subject because it speaks of constant, conscious torment. We must remember, the Good News is that God does not want anyone to go to Hell. God loves everyone and wants everyone of us to spend eternity with Him, and not without Him.

"But God commendeth His love toward us, in that,
while we were yet sinners, Christ died for us."
Romans 5:8

God does not send anyone to Hell. An individual chooses Hell when he or she rejects and refuses God's gift of eternal life through Jesus Christ.

"For God so loved the world, that He gave His only begotten Son,
that whosoever believeth in Him should not perish, but have everlasting life.
For God sent not His Son into the world to condemn the world;
but that the world through Him might be saved."
John 3:16,17

"And this is the condemnation, that light is come into the world,
and men loved darkness rather than light, because their deeds were evil."
John 3:19

If you've never received Jesus Christ as your Savior, don't put it off another second!

"Boast not thyself of tomorrow:
for thou knowest not what a day may bring forth."
Proverbs 27:1

Nothing is worth taking the chance of being lost and standing before God without an advocate or defender.

Accept Jesus Christ Today, because Tomorrow may be too late. Bow your head this moment and ask the Lord Jesus Christ to save you. Pray this prayer below, and mean it with all your heart.

"Lord Jesus, I know that I am a sinner. Unless you save me, I am lost forever. I thank You for dying for me on the Cross.

Lord, I come to You now, the best way I know how. Lord, I ask You to save me. By faith, I now receive You into my heart as my Savior.

Fill me with Your Holy Spirit and help me to live for You from this day forward. Thank You Jesus for saving me. In Jesus Name." Amen

If you've prayed this prayer and have accepted Christ as your personal Savior, be sure to tell someone of your decision. I too, would love to hear about it and rejoice with you.

God bless you in your walk with Him.

☞ Email Your Testimony to: *leroyfreeman@mtcm.com*

25

Quotes & Short Stories

Death is not a period but a comma in the story of life.

♦

A skeptic once derided a Christian man by asking him: "Say, George, what would you say if when you die you found there wasn't such a place as Heaven after all? With a smile the believer replied: "I should say – well, I've had a fine time getting there anyway!" Then the Christian sent a boomerang back to the skeptic – a question not quite so easy to answer. "I say, Fred," he asked, "what would you say if, when you die; you found there was such a place as Hell after all?" - Free Methodist

♦

The nearer the time comes for our departure from this life,
the greater our regret for wasting so much of it.

♦

As a tree falls so must it lie,
As a man lives so must he die,
As a man dies so must he be,
All through the days of eternity.

So live that when death comes
the mourners will outnumber the cheering section.

♦

A little girl whose baby brother had just died asked her mother where the baby had gone. "To be with Jesus," replied the mother. A few days later, talking to a friend, the mother said, "I am so grieved to have lost my baby." The little girl heard her, and, remembering what her mother had told her, looked up to her and asked, "Mother, is a thing lost when you know where it is?" "No, of course not." "Well, then, how can the baby be lost when he has gone to be with Jesus?" Her mother never forgot this. It was the truth.
– Junior King's Business

♦

When we die, we leave behind us
all that we have and take with us, all that we are.

♦

In this dark world of sin and pain,
We only meet to part again;
But when we reach the heavenly shore,
We there shall meet to part no more;
The joy that we shall see that day,
Shall chase our present griefs away.

♦

Jesus bore our sins. When one says, "No" to Jesus Christ,
you're telling God, I don't need Jesus Christ, I'll pay for my own sins.

♦

You tell me you don't believe in Hell;
let me tell you that one second after you've been there, you will.

♦

We are told the wages of sin is death – shouldn't you quit before payday?

A story is told of a poor boy in London. His parents were dead, and he was the charge of a terrible drunken woman, who forced him to beg, and met him with kicks and cuffs if he brought her too little. His greatest pleasure in life was to see the beautiful things exhibited in shop windows. He knew, though, that these things were not meant for him, for there was always the glass between, and he became reconciled to the thought that he could never have them. The lead soldiers had focused his longing for them - but there was the glass.

Alas, he was run over, carried to the hospital, and cared for by a Christian charity. He awoke to find himself in a snow-white cot, and he looked into the pleasant face of a nurse. A few days passed, and then to his astonishment, he saw other children playing with toys. Soon, he sat up in bed, propped up by pillows, and, wonder of wonders, at his hand was a box of lead soldiers. Slowly, he stretched his hand out, touched them, and cried out; "There is no glass between." How will it seem when in the Glory, we no longer see "through a glass, darkly"? - The Expositor

◆

There is a way to stay out of Hell, but no way to get out.

◆

Life with Christ is an endless hope; without Him it is a hopeless end.

◆

William Barclay tells of an old man who, as he lay near death, was obviously troubled. When asked what was disturbing him, replied, "One day when I was young, I was playing with some other boys at a crossroad. We reversed a sign post so that its arms were pointing in the wrong direction, and I've never ceased to wonder how many people were sent in the wrong direction by what we did." - Charles N. Pickell

No man ever repented of being a Christian on his death-bed.

–Hannah More

♦

A fellow said to me on the train one day, "Oh, you preachers make me sick." "I am not a preacher," I replied; "I wish I were. I don't know enough." He said, I don't care what you are. You Christians are always talking about a man going to Hell because Adam sinned." "No," I said, "you will never go to Hell because Adam sinned. You will go to Hell because you refuse the remedy provided for Adam's sin. Don't you go to crying about something that has absolutely been taken care of. If you go to Hell, you will go over the broken body of Jesus Christ who died to keep you out."

- From The Double Cure

♦

The one thing certain about life is that we must leave it.

♦

He who is on the road to heaven will not be content to go there alone.

♦

When that great Christian and scientist Sir Michael Faraday, was dying, some journalist questioned him as to his speculations for a life after death. "Speculations!" said he. "I know nothing about speculations. I'm resting on certainties. "I know that my Redeemer liveth and because He lives, I shall live also." - Gospel Trumpet

♦

No one is dead as long as he is remembered by someone.

"You're just out of date," said young Pastor Bate to one of our faithful old preachers who had carried for years, in travail and tears, the Gospel to poor sinful creatures. "You still preach on Hades, and shock cultured ladies, with your barbarous doctrine of blood. You're so far behind, you will never catch up; you're a flat tire, stuck in the mud." For some little while a wee bit of a smile enlightened the old pastor's face. Being made the butt of ridicule's cut did not ruffle his sweetness or grace. Then he turned to young Bate, so suave and said, "Catch up, did you say? Well, I couldn't succeed if I doubled my speed. My friend, I'm not going your way!"
- Christian Victory

◆

One of the horrors of Hell is the undying memory of a misspent life – "Son, remember." Luke 16:25

◆

"I'm tired of all this preaching about the hereafter," said one. "I'm living now, and I mean to have a good time. The hereafter isn't here yet." Her companion said: "No, only the first part of it. But I shouldn't wonder if the *here* had a good deal to do with shaping the *after*." - Forward

◆

Here is an Ad from the Bible:

- Beautiful New Mansions in a Perfect City
- FREE - 100% Pure Water of Life
- FREE - Utilities - The Lights will never be turned off
- Perfect Society - No need to ever lock your doors
- Beautiful Music always playing
- Ever Bearing Fruit Tree - Perfect Health
- Streets of Gold - Free Transportation
- ... much, much more

Secure a Contract Today for the New Jerusalem

I've purchased a town lot in Heaven, On the city not built with hand.
I'm sending material daily, To build in that happy land.
I'd like a mansion on Main Street, Where streets are all paved with gold.
With a clear view of the pearly gates, Where Christ takes care of the soul.

I want to send good material, That will stand the test of time,
So I'll not be disappointed, When I reach that home sublime.
Prayer is for the foundation, Faith and love for the walls,
Good deeds for the reinforcement, That will stand when the Savior calls.

I would like you for my neighbor, In that city so divine,
Maybe just across the street, Or your home close to mine.
Up there we will know no sorrow, Tears will never dim the eyes,
There we will rest in peace forever, In that happy home on high.

So my friends, start to building, Your home beyond the sky,
Where we can all be together, In the sweet by and by. – Author Unknown

♦

What can it mean to be like Him?
I, to be like my dear Lord?
I could not believe it, had I not
The promise of His precious Word.

I, with follies and failures,
I, with my weakness and sin,
To be like the Lord in His beauty,
Perfect without and within?

He, whom the angels, adoring.
Veil from His glory their eyes.
He, who one glad day will take me
To dwell in His home in the skies?

O, I am weary with waiting:
Sick of this old self of mine:
Come quickly, Lord Jesus, come quickly.
And give me a spirit like Thine. – Martha Snell Nicholson

♦

I've a home prepared where the saints abide,
Just over in the glory land;
And I long to be by my Savior's side,
Just over in the glory land.

Refrain:
Just over in the glory land,
I'll join the happy angel band,
Just over in the glory land;
Just over in the glory land,
There with the mighty host I'll stand,
Just over in the glory land.

I am on my way to those mansions fair,
Just over in the glory land;
There to sing God's praise and His glory share,
Just over in the glory land.

What a joyful thought that my Lord I'll see,
Just over in the glory land;
And with kindred saved, there forever be,
Just over in the glory land.

With the blood-washed throng I will shout and sing,
Just over in the glory land;
Glad hosannas to Christ, the Lord and King,
Just over in the glory land.

James W. Acuff

❖

Sources

1. Gesenius Hebrew And Chaldee Lexicon To The Old Testament Scriptures, Samuel Prideaux Tregelles, LL.D., Copyright 1979, Baker Book House Company

2. The Interlinear KJV-NIV Parallel New Testament In Greek and English, Alfred Marshall, Zondervan Publishing House 1975

3. Thayer's Greek English Lexicon Of The New Testament, Copyright 1977, Joseph Henry Thayer, Baker Book House

4. The New Strong's Exhaustive Concordance Of The Bible, James Strong, LL.D., S.T.D, Copyright 1990, Thomas Nelson Publishers

5. The American Heritage Dictionary (Second College Edition), Copyright 1982, by Houghton Mifflin Company

6. Webster's New World Thesaurus Revised Edition, Copyright 1985, by Simon & Schuster, Inc.

7. Davis Dictionary of the Bible (Fourth Revised Edition), 1978, John D. Davis, Baker Book House

8. An Expository Dictionary Of New Testament Word, W.E. Vine, M.A., Thomas Nelson, Publishers

9. http://www.blueletterbible.org/index.cfm

10. Encyclopedia Of 7,700 Illustrations, Copyright 1979, Paul Lee Tan

11. Good News Bible (The Bible in Today's English Version, Copyright 1976, Thomas Nelson, Publishers

12. Knights Master Book of New Illustrations, Walter B. Knight, Copyright 1956, Wm. B. Eerdmans Publishing

13. http://www.ipsos-na.com/news-polls/reuters-polls/

14. Holy Bible, New Living Translation, Copyright 1996, Tyndale Charitable Trust

15. The Jerusalem Bible (Reader's Edition), Copyright 1968, by Doubleday

Answer Key

Chapter 1 - Questions Concerning Death and The Afterlife

1. Secret, revealed
2. b
3. c
4. Truth
5. Prove all, I Thess. 5:21
6. c
7. John 17:17, Thy [God's] Word
8. d
9. c
10. a

Chapter 2 - Where Did Death Come From?

1. Dress, keep
2. Knowledge of good and of evil
3. d
4. Physical, spiritual, eternal (second)
5. c
6. b
7. c
8. a
9. Physical life
10. "... Ye shall not surely die."

Chapter 3 - Jesus' Victory Over Death

1. A. Destroy the works of the devil, B. Reconcile us back to God
2. d
3. tomb, dead and buried, four
4. come forth, dead came forth, graveclothes, napkin, loose him
5. 500
6. b - - Jesus arose with flesh and bones NOT flesh and blood
7. c
8. Roman
9. a
10. dead, alive, keys, Hell, death
11. e
12. a. meet the full penalty of the law
    b. voluntarily offer to take the sinner's place
    c. die the sinner's death

Chapter 4 - Physical Death of The Body

1. body, soul, spirit
2. d
3. a
4. a
5. 2 Corinthians 5:1
6. souls, bodies
7. terminates, physical
8. d
9. b - - born corruptible NOT incorruptible
10. Verse 23

Chapter 5 - Soul ~ As Used In Scripture

1. b
2. d
3. d
4. d
5. c
6. c
7. a
8. Earthly Desires
9. d
10. Inner Life (the immaterial, invisible part of man)

Chapter 6 - Spirit ~ As Used In Scripture

1. Animals, humans
2. d
3. b
4. Five senses (sight, touch, taste, hearing, smelling)
5. a
6. d
7. d
8. outward man, inward man, 16
9. b - - the correct word is "eso"
10. b - - The Spirit itself beareth witness with (Our spirit) NOT the Holy Spirit

Chapter 7 - Soul Sleep - Truth or Error?

1. a
2. comparing, spiritual things
3. b
4. b
5. knowledge, wisdom, understanding
6. e
7. Ecclesiastes 12:5, 7, 14
8. b
9. a - - (see last page of chapter)
10. c

Chapter 8 - Life After Death

1. a
2. Paul
3. d
4. c
5. d
6. Matthew 10:28
7. comma
8. b - - Jesus descended before He ascended
9. My saying, see death. See my day: saw it
10. Receive my spirit

Chapter 9 - The Spiritual Underworld

1. the devil, his angels
2. cruel, unfair, unloving
3. c
4. a
5. a
6. d
7. The devil himself, ruling, evil empire
8. b and d
9. Sheol, Hades, Gehenna, Tartaroo
10. c, g

Chapter 10 - The Grave

1. c
2. b
3. Sheol
4. Qeber
5. b
6. e
7. b
8. contrasted, equal
9. b - - God said, not Joshua
10. d

Chapter 11 - Hell = Sheol

1. c
2. memory, speech, recognition, communication
3. a
4. Rapha'
5. Nether or underworld, abode
6. temporary place, conscious, disembodied (departed)
7. b
8. c and d
9. a
10. c

Chapter 12 - Hell = Hades

1. Hades
2. d
3. b
4. thanatos
5. heart, three, three
6. a
7. b
8. d
9. separated, spiritual, soul
10. consciousness, physical consciousness

Chapter 13 - Hell = Tartaroo

1. angelic beings
2. Tartaroo
3. Sodom, Gomorrah
4. d
5. c
6. specific compartment, place of confinement, fallen angels, judgment
7. b - -it occurs but once in Scripture
8. Genesis 6:4
9. Verse 6
10. a
11. d - because all are a description of Tartarus

Chapter 14 - Hell = Gehenna

1. b
2. c
3. a
4. b
5. b
6. c
7. a
8. eternal punishment, consequence, wicked
9. Chapter 10, verse 28
10. d
11. c
12. short time, deceive
13. punished, tormented
14. d

15. c
16. Chapter 25, verse 41
17. a
18. books, opened, book, opened, the Book of Life
19. d
20. e

Chapter 15 – Hell = Paradise

1. b
2. c
3. comfort, torment
4. c
5. b - - Acts 2:31 "… His soul was not left in Hell [Hades]"
6. a
7. d
8. c
9. a
10. d
11. temporary
12. f -- (g is incorrect because Ouranos, Shamayim, and the abode of God refer to Heaven above)
13. e
14. c
15. 2 Corinthians, third Heaven

Chapter 16 – The Rich Man & Lazarus

1. b
2. c
3. Abraham's Bosom
4. b
5. testify
6. a
7. functioning consciousness
8. c
9. Luke 16:26
10. D

Chapter 17 – The Resurrection

1. sleeping place
2. d
3. c
4. My Lord, My God
5. a
6. death
7. c
8. b
9. Jesus Christ
10. a
11. Jairus' daughter, Widow's son, Lazarus
12. Death, Hell, the Grave
13. d
14. The Firstfruits
15. d
16. spiritual fellowship, spiritual, physical death
17. c
18. death, mortality, immortality, twinkling
19. a
20. just, unjust
21. suffering
22. c
23. a - - (See Rev. 20:13)
24. offend, cut it off, profitable, into Hell
25. c

Chapter 18 – Heavenly Courtroom

1. judgment
2. b
3. Lord
4. account, deeds
5. d
6. a
7. c
8. fair judgment, Advocate (Intercessor, Defender)
9. righteously
10. d
11. believeth not, condemned, believed
12. Prosecutor, Great White Throne Judgment, waived
13. d
14. Defense Attorney, acquittal
15. a, c, e

Chapter 19 – Degrees of Punishment

1. b
2. prepared, many
3. righteousness
4. terror
5. More Tolerable, Few Stripes, Many Stripes, Greater Damnation
6. d
7. a
8. intentionally, specifics, avoid
9. d
10. works, the deeds

Chapter 20 – Future Rewards

1. b
2. free gift
3. a
4. d
5. b
6. d
7. a
8. b
9. lose, things, full reward
10. d
11. Bema, Bema
12. b - - the believer's sins are judged in this life, but the believer's works will be judged when they stand before Him
13. c
14. endureth temptation, Life
15. d

Chapter 21 – New Heavens & New Earth

1. a
2. remembered, mind
3. b
4. c
5. d
6. a
7. c

8. Second, created, speaking without words
9. first
10. c
11. regeneration
12. regeneration
13. c
14. a
15. foretaste, snapshot

Chapter 22 – The New Jerusalem

1. ages, exceeding riches
2. c
3. d
4. b
5. b
6. presence, joy, pleasures
7. d
8. a -- 216 ft = 144 cubits
9. e
10. “My Father’s House”, unimaginable
11. 4, 17
12. e
13. b -- see Revelation 21:22
14. physical, glorified bodies
15. 17, 4
16. c
17. c
18. b -- the correct scripture is Revelation 22:4
19. a
20. a
21. a
22. glorified bodies, appetite, not be
23. marry, in marriage, neither marry, in marriage, die, the angels
24. sinful, tap or compare
25. Finished

❖

About the Author

Evangelist Leroy Freeman is a native of West Palm Beach, Florida. He was converted to Jesus Christ at the age of 21. He has been proclaiming the Gospel for over 30 years.

Evangelist Freeman is an anointed preacher and teacher of the Word of God who believes in the simplicity of the Gospel. Many call him "The Bag Preacher" because he ministers in a unique way - often times using simple visual illustrations to paint pictures of many Bible truths.

His ministry ministers to both the sheep (mature) and especially the lambs (young). Much of his emphasis is placed on Evangelism and Discipleship as he ever strives to win the lost and prepare all for the soon return of the Lord Jesus Christ.

Leroy Freeman *(Evangelist / Author / Bible Teacher)*

- President of The Leroy Freeman Evangelistic Association, Inc. *(More Than Conquerors)*
- Co-Owner of Rejoice Printing
- KAIROS Prison Ministry Yearly *(Participating Clergy)*
- Emmaus Men's Walk #57 - De Colores!
- Full Gospel Fellowship of Churches and Ministers International member *(since 1999)*

Evangelist Leroy Freeman has been married to Patricia A. Freeman for over 34 years and has three children - LeRoy Jr., Angel, and Gabriel, and a few very lovely grandchildren.

Anointed † Engaging † Inspiring † Motivating

For your next event, contact Evangelist Freeman for speaking availability.

561-329-0173 ~ leroyfreeman@mtcm.com

http://mtcm.com ~ http://leroyfreeman.com

Other Writings

by Leroy Freeman

Very Inspirational - Solid Biblical Advice - Easy To Read

✞

Freedom From Fear and Worry (Surviving The Storm)

Now Available ~ Order Today

- Learn the true MEANING OF FEAR ... Ch. 1
- Learn how to FACE YOUR FEARS ... Ch. 6
- My PERSONAL FEAR REVEALED ... Ch. 8
- Learn the ANTIDOTE FOR FEAR ... Ch. 9
- Learn WHY PEOPLE WORRY .... Ch. 14
- Understanding WORRY vs. FAITH.... Ch. 15
- Learn how to Survive The Storm .... Ch. 21

♦

COMING SOON ~ Test Your Knowledge
Revised Study Edition with Questions and Answers

11 Evidences of Eternal Salvation

At salvation, by the power of the Holy Spirit many things are activated in the new believer's life. Many believers (especially new believers) are not aware of the many workings of the Holy Spirit within them.

In this book, you will see - 11 Evidences of Eternal Salvation. It is impossible to consistently FAKE these Scriptural evidences.

Examine Yourself - Do "U" have them?

COMING SOON ~ Test Your Knowledge
Revised Study Edition with Questions and Answers

Nuggets For Christian Singles
(The Battles, Blessings, and Benefits of Being Single)

The Lord cares about every area of our lives and has much to say about the Season of Singleness.

The world has many counterfeit solutions for Singles that provide temporary relief and often leave the individual worse off than before. This book takes a closer look at God's perspective for Singles.

This is NOT a book about Matchmaking or Dating, but focuses on singles and their relationship with Jesus Christ.

Married couples will benefit from this book as well.

♦

COMING SOON ~ Test Your Knowledge
Revised Study Edition with Questions and Answers

Whole Armor of God
(Are You Properly Dressed?)

There will be many spiritual battles we must fight (against) Satan and his wicked host. We need not fear this conflict because God has provided us with spiritual armor.

There are 7 Pieces of Armor and each piece is for a specific purpose. In order to walk in daily victory and have an abundant life, we must be properly dressed spiritually.

This book describes each piece of the Armor of God and HOW To use them in Spiritual Warfare.

See Website ~ http://mtcm.com ~ For More Details

Notes

❖

www.ingramcontent.com/pod-product-compliance
Lightning Source LLC
Chambersburg PA
CBHW070952040426
42443CB00007B/472

* 9 7 8 0 9 8 2 2 7 3 9 3 7 *